Letters from the Carnival of Death

Correspondence from three of Terry's Texas Rangers

Pauline S. Goldmann

Edited by Michelle M. Haas

Copano Bay Press
2008

Originally published in 1930 under the title *Letters From Three of Terry's Texas Rangers, 1861-1865* as the M.A. thesis of P. S. Goldmann.

ISBN: 978-0-9822467-1-9

This copy of *Letters From The Carnival Of Death*
is part of a limited edition of 254 copies
of which this is No. _________

Contents

PUBLISHER'S NOTE

The boys from Hill's Prairie, through the letters contained in this volume, provide the modern Texas reader with valuable insights into war, peace, sense of place, hope, loyalty, patriotism, slavery and, of course, *spelling and grammar*. From an editorial perspective it was naturally important that this book preserve intact the individual voices of each writer so that we might understand how each might have spoken, how educated each was, etc. Determining how best to preserve the writer's voice while creating a readable text is ever the editor's challenge.

In the case of the letters presented here, stray commas, intermittently poor grammar, obsolete English spellings mixed with modern ones, missing words, unfamiliar slang, common 19th century manuscript abbreviations and a multitude of other anomalies leapt off of each page. The text you find here is a compromise of sorts between the gallant Hill boys and myself. When a misspelling, bygone spelling or awkward sentence structure interfered drastically with how (or whether) a sentence might be read, minor changes were made. Readable sentences with errors were left as they were originally written. The Hill soldiers apologized frequently in their letters home for any mistakes that were made in their writing. I'd like to think they'd be pleased to know that their words have polished up a bit but are still very much their own.

Michelle M. Haas, Managing Editor
Seven Palms - Rockport, Texas

Preface

The Hill letters were written by John, Robert and Dionysius Oliver (D. O.) Hill during the War Between the States to Mary Scott Hill, my grandmother. In editing these letters, I have tried as nearly as possible to identify, in some way, each name which is mentioned. As the letters were written almost seventy years ago, there are a few names which could not be identified.

I am deeply grateful to Dr. Barker for his assistance and for his kindly criticism of this manuscript. I am also grateful for assistance rendered by Mr. T. O. Hill and Mr. Donald Joseph. I wish also to express my appreciation to my grandmother, Mrs. Scottie Williams, my mother, Mrs. Paul H. Goldmann, and to my sister, Mary Goldmann, who have always encouraged me in my work, and for their many helpful suggestions in the writing of this paper.

Pauline Goldmann
May 18, 1930

Part One

Mary Scott Hill

Steward of These Letters

Mary Scott Hill Williams, the recipient and preserver of the letters in this collection, was born at Hill's Prairie, Bastrop County, Texas on July 25th, 1844. She was the seventh child of Julia Foster Walker and Middleton Milledge Hill, the founders of Hill's Prairie. The day of the birth of Mary Scott was one of rejoicing; the horns on the plantation were blown to call the slaves to the big house to celebrate the birth of the first dark-eyed baby to the Hill family.

Mary Scott grew up in a well-regulated and almost independent little kingdom. She was much beloved by her brothers, as is evidenced by these letters. Her early education was obtained in the little log school house, erected and maintained by the Hill family and their neighbors. She was taught her ABC's, and she learned to write by first making the famous "pot hooks," which were practiced by beginners before they were considered expert enough to attempt real penmanship. At home, she learned to spin and weave, and was taught the daintiest and most exquisite needlework. At twelve years of age, she was sent to Bastrop to a school maintained by Revered Mr. Thrall to begin her higher education. It was here that she studied mathematics, Latin, astronomy, botany, rhetoric and philosophy. She also attended dancing school. Later, Mary Scott was sent to Rutersville College, where her older sisters Sarah and Martha Hill had each received their education.

During the years of her girlhood, she became a great favorite, and was considered the most beautiful young lady in Bastrop County. At the tournaments, she was voted the favorite and many a young man vied for her colors to wear on his lance.

As Mary Scott grew to young ladyhood she was surrounded by every luxury and comfort found in a southern plantation home. She had her own maid, whose duty it was to "wait on" her young mistress and the young ladies who came to visit in the Hill home. There was constant visiting, back and forth, between the Hill, Oliver and McGehee families, who had been closely connected for generations by ties of friendship and marriage.

Mary Scott rode thirty miles on horseback to see the first cooking stove in that part of the country. She stood in awe, expecting the stove to explode at any minute. The first kerosene lamp was considered a luxury, as previous to this only candles were used. The most outstanding experience of her life was her first long journey from home — a trip by stage to Brenham, where the first railroad in Texas then ended in its western terminal. "Brother John," the writer of many of these letters, took her from Hill's Prairie to Brenham, by stage, then to Houston by train, where they took a boat to Galveston. The boat was commanded by Captain Pat Christian. Mary Scott was honored by being seated at the Captain's right, and many other attentions were shown her. This was a gala event in her life, and one which, in later life, she looked back on with much pleasure.

One of the most notable moments of Mary Scott's life was the witnessing of the inauguration of Sam Houston as governor of Texas. She was attending school at Rutersville when her mother sent for her to accompany the family to Austin to attend the ceremony. The drive to Austin was made in the family carriage, and took all day. The Hills brought one of their fine carriage horses, Black Hawk, which was matched by an equally fine-blooded animal owned by Milas Long. This span of black horses, covered with net and proudly wearing a headdress of plumes, drew the governor's carriage up the Avenue to the old Capitol building, where the inaugural ceremonies were held.

When the Civil War began, Mary Scott went home from school to care for her invalid mother, and to take up the duties which fell to the lot of southern women during the War Between the

States. Mary Scott took complete charge of the plantation, as her father had died many years previous. There were many duties in her charge such as branding the cattle, harvesting the crops, curing the meat, and laying in the winter's supply of food.

The financial burden of managing the affairs of the plantation were stupendous for a girl of the period. One tragedy which came to the young manager was the loss of cotton sent to Brownsville for sale. The man to whom the cotton was entrusted reported the loss of three wagon loads, consisting of twenty-four bales. He also reported that eight yoke of oxen froze to death. However, with undaunted courage, crops were started the next year and were paid for in Confederate money.

Few realize the bravery of this generation of women, who were reared in luxury, yet faced the privations brought on by the war. With courageous hearts, they cheered the returning soldiers, nursed them back to health and helped take up the struggle against the tragic era of Reconstruction.

On July 22, 1869, Mary Scott Hill united in marriage with James Duncan Williams of Fayette County, Texas. He had served as a lieutenant in Green's Brigade from 1861 to 1865. This young couple lived for many years at the Williams plantation in the old Williams home, two and one-half miles east of Winchester. They later moved to Giddings to educate the two children born to them— Julia Miles Williams and Mamie Duncan Williams.

James Duncan Williams died in 1892 and was buried in Brenham, Texas. Mary Scott, left a widow, lived in Giddings until February 19, 1905, when she moved with her son–in–law and daughter, Mr. and Mrs. Paul H. Goldmann, to Austin.

It was through the efforts of this remarkable woman that the letters which follow have been preserved. Mary Scott was born in Texas and she lived in Texas under four flags— the flag of the Lone Star, the flag of the United States, the Confederate flag, and again the flag of the United States.

During the writing of this thesis, she has shown an unusual interest, and it is my great sorrow that she did not live to see it in its finished state. Prior to the completion of this thesis, Mary Scott Hill slept her last sleep March 20, 1930, at her home in Austin. She was buried in the State Cemetery.

Part Two

A Brief History of Terry's Texas Rangers

The Secession Convention was held in Austin in March, 1861. Among the delegates at this convention were Thomas Lubbock, a commission merchant of Houston; his kinsman, B. F. Terry, a sugar planter of Fort Bend County; and John Wharton, a native Texan, planter and lawyer of Brazoria. At the close of the Convention, they were returning to their homes by stage and had ample time to discuss the events then transpiring, the underlying causes of the Convention, and the war clouds which were gathering over the South. They decided to rush to Montgomery, Alabama, to offer their services to President Jefferson Davis. They returned to their homes and made all necessary arrangements for immediate departure. Terry and Lubbock went overland. Wharton went by the Gulf, as he thought the trip could be made in less time. Wharton was captured.

Terry and Lubbock arrived in Montgomery and were sent to Virginia, where General Longstreet was preparing for the First Manassas, and arrived in time to participate in this battle. They served with distinction as is shown by the fact that General Beauregard said in his official report of the engagement:

> ...finds it proper to acknowledge the signal services rendered by Colonels B. F. Terry and T. Lubbock of Texas. They made valuable reconnaissance of the enemy's position and carried orders to the field. Colonel Terry, with his unerring rifle, severed the halyard, and thus lowered the Federal flag floating on the courthouse, and also secured a large Federal garrison flag, designed, it is said, to be unfurled over our intrenchments at Manassas.[1]

1. D. G. Wooten, *A Comprehensive History of Texas,* II, 682.

In recognition of the services rendered, Terry and Lubbock received their commissions, and returned to Texas to recruit a cavalry regiment for service in Virginia. Headquarters were established at Houston, and through the newspapers of Texas the following call for volunteers was issued:

> August 12, 1861
>
> Having been authorized by the Secretary of War of the Confederate States of America to raise a regiment of mounted rangers for service in Virginia, we hereby appoint Captain —— to raise and enroll a full company, to consist of one captain, one first lieutenant, two second lieutenants, four corporals, one blacksmith, two musicians, and from sixty-four to one hundred privates, and to report the same to use on or before the 1st of September next. Each man will be required to furnish equipment for his horse and to arm himself. The company will be transported free. The term of service will be during the war unless sooner discharged.
>
> B. F. Terry.
> T. S. Lubbock[2]

Within less than a month, the recruits were on their way to Houston, the central point of mobilization. On September 9, 1861, ten companies of one hundred men each were mustered into service, swearing to serve until the end of the war. The personnel of the regiment consisted of men from the leading families of Texas. Many of the volunteers, in their teens and early twenties, were college graduates, professional men, merchants, farmers and stockmen—most of whom were excellent shots and expert horsemen. Their main desire was to get to the war as members of a crack cavalry troop before the war was over.

2. D. G. Wooten, *A Comprehensive History of Texas,* II, 683.

Colonel Terry rode down the streets of Houston, with his daughter Cordelia Terry (Mrs. William Thatcher of Austin) on his shoulder, leading his regiment. Amid flags flying, bugles blowing, tearful sweethearts and wives bidding a last farewell to the soldiers, the journey to Virginia was begun. On September 11, 1861, the La Grange company left for the front—followed by the Brazoria Company and the Bastrop Company commanded by John Wharton. The journey to the war was undertaken at last.

The following are the companies with the names of their captains and the counties from which they were recruited:

Company A	Thomas Harrison	McLennan & adjoining Counties.
Company B	John A. Wharton	Brazoria and Matagorda Counties
Company C	Mark Evans	Gonzales and adjoining Counties
Company D	Steve Ferrell	Bastrop, Hayes, Travis and Burleson Counties.
Company E	L. W. Rayburn	Gonzales and adjoining Counties.
Company F	Louis M. Strobel	Fayette County.
Company G	W. Y. Houston	Bexar & Goliad Counties.
Company H	John T. Holt	Fort Bend County
Company I	J. G. Jones	Gonzales and adjoining Counties.
Company K	John G. Walker	Harris and Montgomery Counties.

From Houston to Beaumont over a newly constructed railroad, it took nearly all day to make eighty miles. From Beaumont, by steamboat, down the Neches and up the Sabine to Niblett's Bluff; thence a hundred miles on foot,

> through water much of the way; thence forty miles in carts. It is easy to remember this cart ride. The wheels were six or seven feet high. Motive power, oxen, two pairs of each cart. Engineers, little bow–legged Creoles, each armed with a long, sharp–pointed pole. The vehicles had no springs. As there were no seats, the six or eight passengers in each conveyance had to stand on their feet. At New Iberia, on Bayou Teche, we were transferred to boats, and went down between the beautiful banks of that stream to Brashear, now Morgan City. From there we went through an almost continuous sugar farm to New Orleans. The trip from Houston to New Orleans took over a week. It is now made in less than twelve hours, in a palace car.[3]

At New Orleans, Colonel Terry received a letter from General Albert Sidney Johnston, then recruiting an army at Bowling Green, Kentucky, for defense of the frontier. He requested the Rangers to join him there, promising that while under him they should remain an independent command. A vote of the regiment was taken, and, as General Johnston was a former Texan and personally known to many members, Kentucky was chosen as their destination. They traveled in box cars, previously used for shipping cattle. When the Rangers reach Nashville, who later presented them with a beautiful silk flag. From Nashville, Colonel Terry was ordered to Bowling Green and there the companies were formally organized into a regiment and mustered into service as the Eighth Texas Cavalry, better known to history and fame as Terry's Texas Rangers.

The following officers were elected:

B. F. Terry, Colonel
Thomas S. Lubbock, Lieutenant-Colonel
Thomas Harrison, Major.

---

3. L. B. Giles, *Terry's Texas Rangers*, 16-17

The following staff officers were appointed:

M. H. Royston, Adjutant
B. H. Botts, Quarter–Master
Robert Summons, Commissary
R. F. Buntin, Chaplain
W. D. Manning, Surgeon
Robert E. Hill, Assistant Surgeon
W. B. Sayers, Sergeant Major
Thomas J. Potts, Hospital Steward
James Edmondson, Ordinance Sergeant
M. F. Deballegathy, Quartermaster Sergeant

At Woodsonville, Kentucky, December 17, 1861, the Rangers made their first charge, losing their gallant leader, Colonel Terry. General Hardee says of this charge:

> The conduct of the Rangers was marked by impetuous valor. In charging the enemy, Colonel Terry was killed in the moment of victory. His regiment deplores the loss of a beloved and brave commander, the army one of its ablest officers.[4]

Lieutenant–Colonel Lubbock, though ill with typhoid fever at Nashville, was elected to fill Colonel Terry's place. Lubbock died a few days later, and John A. Wharton was advanced to the command of the regiment.

Terry's Texas Rangers served under many eminent officers; among them were Terry, Wharton, Harrison, Hardee, Albert Sidney Johnston, Longstreet, Bragg, Wheeler, Forrest, Joseph E. Johnston, Hood, Hindman, Lee and Jackson. They participated in many of the most important battles of the War Between the States, including Shiloh, where General Albert S. Johnston was killed, Bardstown, Perryville, Murfreesboro, in the five day's battle, Chickamauga, Knoxville and many other battles which are described in the letters which follow.

---

4. D. G. Wooten (ed.), *A Comprehensive History of Texas*, II, 684.

They surrendered under General Joseph Johnston to Sherman at Greensboro, North Carolina. The following is General Wheeler's last order:

Headquarters Cavalry Corps.
April 28m 1865.

Gallant Comrades: you have fought your fight. Your task is done. During a four years' struggle for liberty you have exhibited courage, fortitude and devotion. You are the victors of more than 200 sternly contested fields. You have participated in more than a thousand conflicts of arms. You are heroes! Veterans! Patriots! The bones of your comrades mark battlefields upon the soil of Kentucky, Virginia, North Carolina, South Carolina, Georgia, Alabama and Mississippi. You have done all that human exertion could accomplish. In bidding you adieu, I desire to tender my thanks for your gallantry in battle, your fortitude under suffering and your devotion at all times to the holy cause you have done so much to maintain. I desire also to express my gratitude for the kind feelings you have seen fit to extend toward myself, and to invoke upon you the blessing of our Heavenly Father, to whom we must always look in the hour of distress. Brethren, in the cause of freedom, comrades in arms, I bid you farewell.

Joseph Wheeler,
Major General

Official:
Wm. E. Waites,
Assistant Adjutant General[5]

There are no more reunions of the noble Terry's Texas Rangers. The few surviving members, at this writing, are in the fourscore

5. L. B. Giles, *Terry's Texas Rangers*, 98-99.

years and more. Those who are left of the original number, who for many years gathered in their annual reunions at Austin, will gather here no more.

Part Three
The Letters

Robert Edward Hill to Mary Scott Hill

Houston Sept 12, 1861

Dear Sister

After having to stay hear untill now; we preparing to leave—we will leave our present quarters this evening and go out to the depot and tomorrow morning will find us nor preventing providence on our journey to Va.

The health of the camp is very good. We have had plenty of good cistern water to drink since we have been here & the Citizens of this place have treated us very well.

The Lagrange Company went yesterday morning & ours will go with the Brazoria Company commanded by John Wharton—when I get to Brashia City if I have time I will write again.

They are going to call the roll & I must stop.

Good by, Love to all,
Bob

John W. Hill to Mary Scott Hill

New Orleans Sept 30, 1861

Miss Scott Hill
Bastrop

Dear Sister

We arrived in this City day before yesterday Safe and Sound. I Have traveled over the City a good deal. Have seen a great many

New and Strange things. I went to the Acadmy of Musick knight before last. Went to church twice yesterday, heard two good Sirmons. There is to be two hundred & fifty Northern Prisners here this morning on the Jackson [Railroad.] There is a great many persons on the streets to witness there arival. We received orders last knight by Telegraph to go to Kentucky instead of Virginia. We will leave here in the morning for Nashvile Tenesee where we will be mounted. There is som dissatisfaction among some of the Companyes as to the change of our servise from Virginia to that of Kentucky. There is four of the Companys that make up the Regment here. The fifthe from La Grange did not stop here though they stoped at the Grand Junction. The other five Companys are on the Road.

Bud McGuire[1] got with us at Houston and is still withe us. He started from Home to join Robinson's Company of Infantry. Butt iff he can git a sadle and Six-Shooter I guess that he will stay with our Company in the plase of Robert Ship[2] who was sick and [who] we had to leave on the Road. His Brother Oliver was left behind with him. He got here yesterday And reports Bob is better but not able to travle. I have nothing more to write that would interest you. We are all well and getting along well. I would like for you to write to me But I do not know where to tell you to write.

My Love to all and axcept the same yourselfe.

Your Brother,
John W. Hill

1. Bud McGuire- Frank McGuire, who was a nephew of Mrs. Middleton Hill's. He was from Fayette County, Texas, and a member of Terry's Rangers.

2. Robert Ship—a neighbor of the Hills who owned a large plantation just across from the Hill's.

JOHN HILL TO MARY SCOTT HILL

Camp Johnson Nov 14, 1861

Miss M S. Hill
Bastrop

Dear Sister

Your letter came to hand several days ago Butt as it found me down with the measles I have put off writing till now. I was down with the measles for a week and was very sick for several dayes. Butt thank God I am on foot once more and hope to stay so for the balance of the time that I am in service. The Company went out on a scout last Monday and was out five dayes but did not meet up with any of the Enemy. There was about a Dozen of the boyes took the Measles whilest they were out. D. O. Hill[3] was one of the number.

They did not hurt him a bit. He just lay there and whistled & sung as thoug there was nothing the matter. There has a great many of our sick bin sent down to Nashvill. John D Hunt[4] is quite sick as well as Phillip Phillips.[5] Cousin Charley McGehee[6] has also bin quite sick But is improving slowly. One of our companys went out on a scout a few days ago and met up withe the Enemy. They killed two of them, took one prisiner. News came to camp yesterday that Russau has crossed the River and was advancing on this place. But we have had it reported so often that he was coming that we have got so that we don't believe it. I Am beginning to think that we will not have any fighting here this winter. Neither armey show any disposition to advance and will soon be time to go into Winter quarters. They had a fight at Columbus in this state a few days ago But you can learne more from papers than I can write. Charley McGehee got a letter from his brother John at Richmon Va a few days ago. He said in his letter they were having

3. D. O. Hill was a son of T. B. J. Hill, who was a founder of Hill's Prairie.
4. John D. Hunt was from Bastrop.
5. Phillip Phillipe was from Bastrop County
6. Charley McGehee was a third cousin of the Hills. He lived in San Marcos.

a great deale of sickness, about one half of the Regment sick He says that Cousin T. A. Hill[7] was in Richmond about two weeks before he wrote But that he left for North Carolina the next day . Brother Robert and Dr Roiston[8] are bothe acting as assistant Surgeons. They are bothe kept very busey. Brother says that he will write as soon as he has time. Scott you must excuse all mistakes and write a long letter in answer to this. Where is Brother Tom & James?[9] Sister Matt and all the others promised to write to me. I love to read letters better than write them But yours is first since I left. And I have written to all. All the Boyes joine me in love to you all. Tell Ma that I hope it will not be many months before we meet again. My Love to all the Neighbors and friends

Your Brother,
John W. Hill

7. T. A. Hill was a brother of D. O. Hill. He was not a member of Terry's Texas Rangers as he was in Georgia when the war broke out, and he enlisted with a Georgia regiment.
8. Dr. Roiston lived in Hill's Prairie. He married a first cousin of D. O. Hill.
9. Brother Tom and James were sons of Middleton Hill, and brothers of John Hill. Sister Matt was Martha Hill.

John W. Hill to Mary Scott Hill

Camp Cave City Dec 19, 1861

Miss. M. S. Hill
Bastrop

Dear Sister

Yours and Bro James letter of the first of this month came to hand yesterday. I was very glad to hear that you were all well. When I wrote my last letter to Bro Thomas we were about leaving on a scout. Since that time we have bin traveling nearly all the time, for the first week we spent in taking Horses, Beef Cattle, Hogs and Everything that we could use to an advantage from the Union men in this country. On last Sunday we went up to Woodsvill, a town on Green River where the Enemy has a large forse on the other side. We found a lot of the Enemys Picket on this side of the River. We pitched into them and wounded two and took one other prisnor and run the others into town where they had a large forse. On last Tuesday Col. Terry [left] with Eight parts of Companys, for there is yet a great many sick, withe about eleven hundred of Genl Hindmans infantry. Went up to the same place withe the intention of trying to drive them back across the River. This is the place that the Louisvill and Nasvill Rail Road crosses Green River. When they arived at Rowlets Station one and half miles from town they come in sight of the enemy. They were drawn up in line of Battle on a hill in a thick woods on bothe sides of the Road. Instead of bringing on the atack withe the Infantry and driving them off of the hill into and open field, Capt Ferril & Holt was plaised on the Right while Terry and the other companys on the left. The order was given to charge and Sutch a charge I do not Supose was ever made before. Four or five hundred cavalry charging; some say two, some more Regments of Infantry where they had trees, fences and Ditches along the Rail Road to fall behind. But they pourd the shot and Six Shooter balls into us. While we gave back, the miney Balls came like bees. But we drove them back and when we got them into the field we gave it to them heavy.

Col Terry[10] was killed in the first charge. There was two killed out of our Company, Frank Lofton[11] and Gov Bell that lived over the River at Mr Nunns. We had four wounded: A young man, Lue Giles[12] the Dr does not think will live; another young man by the name of Giles was wounded Slightly; John Henry,[13] Slightly; Sam Friedbarger[14] broke his Collar Bone by the falling of his horse when the Horse was shot. Capt Walker lost one man. His 1st Leut was badly wounded. One other was shot through bothe armes but not dangerous. There was one or two slightly wound in Wharttons company. There was a good many horses killed. There was but few of the Infantrey that were in the action.

After the Enemy were driven back across the field our Regiment was ordered back to give the Artilery a chance. We had four Brass pieces. We gave it to them till they begun to recive reinforcements in large numbers and Genl Hindman gave orders for us to fall back. Now as to myself, a few dayes ago, I was apointed fourth Sargent by Capt Feril. On Tuesday there was a Sargent required from our Company to take charge of the waggon Gard So you see that I was not withe [the] company in the fight, but was off some three or four hundred yards. I cant describe my feelings when I saw the Enemy and Saw our Boyes charging them. Then here come one of Walkers men withe a young man behind him wounded through bothe armes. Then the news that Col Terry had fallen. The Infantry running to and from the waggons and the Guard begging for Gods Sak[e] to let them go. But like the Sailor Boy I was determined not to desirt my post though I would have given my all to have bin withe my Company. We took the

10. Colonel Terry was the organizer of the regiment.

11. Frank Lofton and Gov. Bell were from Bastrop. They lived at Mrs. Nunn's, who had a farm a short distance from the Hill home.

12. Lue Giles was from Travis County

13. John Henry was from Travis County

14. Sam Friedbarger was from Bastrop.

Waggons along Expecting to drive them across the river but they had two many on this sid[e] so we had to fall back to this place which is Eight miles from the River. There is about four thousand troops here and we are looking for reinforcements. Bob Hill[15] and Bro Bob was in the fight. Cap[16] did not come withe us. He had some biles and could not ride. I heard from him yesterday and he was gitting better. Dick Roiston's healthe is bad. I heard a few dayes ago that he had aplied for a Discharge. Charly Morgan[17] has got a discharge and left us yesterday for home. He is going to take Johns[18] Remains withe him. Col Terrys remains were taken home. The Enemeys loss is Estimated at from fifty to one hundred and twenty five.

We are camped in Six miles of Mamouth Cave. You must Excuse this for I have to use my cart[ridge] box for a writing desk. You must give my kindest regards to all the neighbors. You all give it to me for not writing. Last week is the first week that I have missed in a long while. I have written Sister Matt, T. Brooks[19] Bro Tom, Jim,[20] you, Sister Sarah and all the rest. We have bin having the finest weather I ever Saw. Dayes are warme and pleasant while the knights are cold. Write Soon and a heap of it. You & Jim did not fill two pages but I shall not grumble iff it is only a line. You all must not wait for me to wright for I will eavry chance

Your Brother,
John. W. Hill

Direct letters to Bowling Green Ky

---

15. Bob Hill was a son of Wylie Hill, who was one of the founders of Hill's Prairie.
16. Cap was D. O. Hill
17. Charley Morgan was from Bastrop, Texas.
18. John was John Morgan, a brother of Charley.
19. T. Brooks was the husband of Martha Hill, who was a sister of the writer of this letter.
20. A reference to his brothers and sisters.

ROBERT EDWARD HILL TO MARY SCOTT HILL

Camp Oakland Dec 22, 1861

Dear Sister

It has been so long since I wrote that I had almost concluded that I was entirely out of practice. The last letter I wrote was to Cousin Nish[21] whilst I was down at our other encampment, near Bowling Green. We were ordered out here to this place which was the advance post, 10 or 12 miles in advance of any of the troops.

On last Monday that was two weeks ago. We were ordered to have 7 days provisions prepared and we started on a trip toward the Yankees. We went on untill we got to Green River at a place called Woodsonvill or Mumfordsvill. There are two places one on each side of the river, only the river between them. The Yankees are encamped at Mumfordsvill. We saw their tents and could see them walking about their camps. There were more on this side of the river. We found out that they were making boats and bridges to cross on this side we came back and camped about 10 miles from this river. On the Sunday following we went up there again and found some on this side of the river. We shot two of them and took one prisoner. On last Tuesday we went up there with some infantry troops to tear up the railroad track. When we arrived at the place where we had fought them on Sunday we could see them moving in large bodies. They came out to meet us and Col. Terry ordered a charge when our boys raised a shout that for a while drowned the reports of the guns. They dashed right into them and began shooting and the Yankees began to run. Our brave Col. was killed while leading his men on. We had 2 killed in our company. One named Frank Loftin and W. W. Bell.[22] Cousin Nish knows both of them well. You can tell Cousin Nish that the Gov. Bell was shot twice once almost right through the region of

---

21. Cousin Nish was Dionysius Oliver, who was a brother of Mrs. T. B. J. Hill. He lived in Bastrop.

22. W. W. Bell was from Bastrop County.

the heart and the other shot in the leg which almost cut it off. I did not get to see Bell. I was busy with some of the boys that was wounded trying to get them off [the field] and get their wounds dressed. Bell & Loftin were killed and two men [named] Giles and one by the name of John Henry were wounded in our Comp. Capt. Walker lost one man and had 3 wounded. Sam Fredbarger had his horse killed and in the fall Sam had his collar bone broken. We then came back to where our camp was and ever since then we have been on the alert hardly sleeping or eating. Our horses have been sadeled more than half the time and the men prepared to spring into the sadel at a moments warning.

Nearly their whole army are dutch that have been here only a few years. Every one that we have taken prisoner is dutch and they have joined to keep their families from suffering that they could not get anything to do and they could not let their fraus starve to death. We captured several letters the other day with the knapsacks and they were from dutch women living in Cincinatti all begging their husbands to send them some money, that what they could get there did not pay the rents and they would be turned out of doors if they did not pay up. It is perfectly outrageous that we have to fight such material whilst those vile abolitionists that have brought and urged this war on should be securely left at home.

Our Comp has had a great deal of sickness and some deaths. John Morgan died at Nashvill sometime ago. I could not get down to see him. Brother John, Cap and Bob and myself are all up. Dr. Royston and Dick[23] are both sick and I reckon will both go down to Missipii or come home. If they stay here they will both die.

Tell Cousin Nish that Ben Toliver that lived in Missipi is captain in an Arkansas Company and sends his love to all the relations that live in Texas. He has two Brothers and one Uncle in Genl Hindmans Brigade. Our Regiment is attached to the same Bri-

---

23. Dick Roiston was a brother of Dr. Roiston, who has been mentioned. They lived in Hill's Prairie.

gade. They are all from Arkansas and are the keenest men for a fight I nearly ever saw

Tell Uncle Tom[24] that I would have written to him again but I have been eating and sleeping almost constantly in the saddle for the last 17 days and would now be up where our Comp is, but Dr Royston is sick and not able to attend the sick and I had to come down and take charge of them. I will write oftener if I remain here and keep you all posted with what is going on in this part of Kentucky which is to be emphatically the Dark and bloody ground.

We heard the other day that Galveston was burned to the ground and you can have no ideas of my feelings. I thought that my own loved state was to be invaded and I here in Kentucky fighting those confounded dutch.

Say to Cousin Nish that John Hunt had his papers all fixed up for a discharge from service and when I started on our last trip expected that he would be able to start right straight home, but through negligence on the part of those who were in command they were mislaid and John did not get hold of them. I expect to make out new ones for him and thus be will be able to get off in a few days. His health is improving slowly. He is here with me now.

Give my love to all enquiring friends and tell Mother that I never lay down at night without asking the good lord to bless me and keep me untill we all meet at Home around our fireside as we left. I do hope that she may get well and that it may not be long untill we will be all together again.

I think that I have written enough to night so goodby untill you hear from me again.

Your Brother,
Bob

P.S. if you see Miss Mid[25] shortly give her my love and say to her that I often remember her

---

24. Uncle Tom was Thomas Baytop Hill, a brother of Middleton Hill. He was a founder of Hill's Prairie.
25. Miss Mid was Miss Middie Hart from Fayatte County. Her parents lived in Winchester, Texas.

Robert Hill to Mary Scott Hill

Bowling Green Ky, Jan 29, 1862

Dear Sister

The last letter I wrote home was one to Brother Tom from Mr. Alexander's and mailed at Gallatin Tennessee. I came up to this place day before yesterday and have had no way to get up to where our boys [are]. The cars only make occasional trips. They will go up to day or tomorrow. Consequently I do not know how the boys are getting along. I feel that I am getting my strength again and will soon be as well as ever. The weather here is very warm and raining untill it is very unpleasant and I fear [will] cause a great deal of sickness in the camps of our troops. I saw one of our Regiment who came down here on yesterday. He says that our Regiment were camped [with]in 12 miles of the Yankees but he did not think that they were going to advance on us

They are still at work here fortifying this place. It will give the Yankees some Trouble should they attempt to take this place. They may find it a second Manasas.

I received your letter dated January 10 and yesterday got out of the office the one to Brother John of December the 29th so you see the mails are very irregular.

Scott give my love to all enquiring friends and when I get up to the Regiment I will then give you another good long letter.

And will try and get more paper so that I wont have to cross. I Knew Ma would be uneasy when she heard that I was sick so I write this to let her know that I am well enough to again attend to duty.

Bob

D. O. HILL TO MARY SCOTT HILL

Camp Moreing at Bell Tavern, Jan 31, 1862

Miss Scott Hill

Dear Cousin

As I have not stuck to my promise and wrote to you before this time I will now do so and try to be more faithful in the future and all I can do is to ask your forgiveness and to forget the past. This [leaves] John, Bud Mc[Guire] & myself in good health at present except bad colds. Dr & Dick Royston have both got discharges and going home. I believe that Dick has gon down into Mississippi to his sisters but Dr is at home by this time I guess. [You] must excuse the dirt that is on this letter for since I have got into camp you must know that I can not keep as clean as we can at home. But you say that Miss Maggie Johns[26] has taken my ambrotype from you. You say that you want me to send you another. You must tell her to wait until I get home and I will give her the original. Ask her how she would like it. [If she does] tell her to wait until I get there and she can have it. Tell her if she lets a certain young lady see her with my ambrotype she will have a fight on her hands in little of no time. Tell all of the girls that we boys had a fine christmass of it scouting in the rain in an enemies country. I thought on last Wednesday morning that we were in for a fight. We rod[e] up in sight of a body of cavalry but they turned out to be friends they joined us and we then went up to Horse Cave but found nothing. We then started down to a mill and received a dispach from Col Whorton to come home. And then Capt Ferrill and some seven or eight others went up in a mile or two from Green River and were shot and had to turn around and come in to camp. They found out all that they wanted to and came back. General Gallicoffers remains are to pass here to night Scott. If

26. Miss Maggie Johns was a niece of The Reverend I. G. Johns. He was a Methodist minister who lived in Hill's Prairie.

you remember it has been five monthes since I grasped your hand in mine. All of the boys of your acquaintance are in good health. John[27] is feeling weak butt is reading the last Texas papers. Give my love to all of the friends and neighbors and tell me all of the news in your next letter.

I remain as ever your Cousin,
D. O. Hill

Scott you will have to pay postage on my letters for we never see a dime in silver and they wont take paper money for postage

Your Cousin as ever,
D. O. Hill

JOHN W. HILL TO MARY SCOTT HILL

Genrl Hindmans Headquarters
Bells Station Feb 4, 1862

Miss M S Hill

Dear Sister

Yours of the 29th. December was received by me a few days ago. Bro Bob also received one of 10th of last month from you about the same time I am very glad to hear that you are all well and to hear that Ma's leg was improving. Very sorry to hear that you are having so mutch dry weather in Texas. I am very mutch afraid iff you have had no rain up to this date that you will have

27. John was John Hill

a very bad crop year in Texas this year. We have rain here all the time. We have not had but one or two sun shiney days sins about 20th December. It rains two or three days then snows and sleets then rains again. The whole country is a perfect mud hole and the roads are all most impasable. We arrived at this place last Friday was a week ago; we will stay here about five weeks. To give you some idier of what we have to do, I was put on picket guard last Sunday was a week. It rained all knight. Got to camp Monday about twelve o'clock. Tuesday morning started with the Company on a three days Scout. We went up the pike about Eight miles in the direction of Green River; we then turned to the left towards Mamouth cave. Rod[e] over the roughest country I ever saw about five miles whene at the top of a high hill we came in sight of the Enemys camp. There is five Regments about two miles this sid[e] of where we had the fight. As we had only sixty men our company and Capt Wm. R. Jormons company of Fayette Co. we thought it best to let them alone in there glorey. We then came back to Cave Cittey about six miles above this plase, Camped for the knight. It rain all knight and all the next day but the rain did not stop us. We started out the next day with wet blankets, wet gunns and wet selves; rod[e] all day going to Hors-wells Hors-Cave. [At] the last named plase the Enemy have set several traps to catch us but I think we are two old for them. We would have had to lay out another knight had not Col Wharton sent out an order for us to come into camp. Last Saturday I was on picket again. Rained all the time again. And I expect that the Company will be ordered out on another scout tomorrow Cousin T. A. Hill got here day before yesterday. He come up to Bowlin-Green after some two or three men that had left there Battalion and joined some Alabama Regment for twelve months. He got a pass for two dayes and come up to see us. He is in fine healthe and looks better than I ever saw him. He sayes that they are having a very easy time of it at Greensville. Good houses for all of there Companys to stay in. He says that he would like to belong to this Regment iff we did not have sutch a hard time at it. Cap was out on Picket when he came and yesterday eavning till after Tom was gone so Cap did not git to see his Brother. Cap is in fine healthe. Frank had a chill last knight but is up this morning. Wm Simms[28] took the Diahrea very bad after he got to camp and after he come up here the Measils broke out on him. R. T. Hill[29] went withe him to Galtin in Tenn. He is at Mrs. Millers and I expect he is quit[e] sick as Bob Hill has not come back yett. He is at a nise place and they will give him eavrey attention. Brother Bob is in camp but he looks a good deale worsted from the spell that he had. Charley McGehee got his discharge and is at home iff he had good luck. Oliver Ship[30] was a great deal better the last time I heard from him and I guess that he is on his way home before this. There was Eight Prisoners sent from his plase to Bowlin-Green yesterday. They were taken by Capt John Morgan on the other side of Green River. All the boyes of your acquaintance that are in Camp are well. I give Cousin Tom[31] your last letter, Uncle Toms[32] last to Cap and a letter from Cousin Nish as he said that he had not heard from home in some time. You must excuse this for this is the meanest pen that I ever tryed to write with in my life. Give my love to all the Relations and friends and except the same for your selfe. Write soon and a heap of it. Cap, Frank[33] and Bro Bob all send love to you all

Your Brother,
Jno. W. Hill

Why does not Bro Jim write to me ?

---

28. William Simms was from Bastrop, and a member of the Terry Rangers.
29. R. T. Hill was a son of Wiley Hill. He was a first cousin of John and Bob Hill. R. T. Hill is also referred to as Bob Hill. He may be distinguished from Dr. Robert Hill by the fact that throughout these letters Dr. Hill is spoken of as Brother Bob or as Bob, while R. T. Hill is also called or is called Bob Hill.
30. Oliver Ship was a brother of Robert Ship, who was previously mentioned. They lived across the river from the Hills.
31. Cousin Tom was Tom Hill, a brother of D. O. Hill.
32. Uncle Tom was T. B. J. Hill who came to Texas with Middleton Hill.
33. Frank refers to Frank McGuire who has been referred to before.

Robert Hill to Jas. H. Hill[34]

Murfresbourough Tennessee Feb 23, 1862

My Dear Brother

You will no doubt be glad to hear that I am safe in the grand retreat from Bowling Green. We began to retreat from Green River on Sunday the 16th and fell back to bowling Green & found that the army had evacuated the place, and on friday the yanks made their appearance and began to throw shell into the town without giving the citizens any warning. The only damage done was the killing of one woman as I have since learned. We left Bowling Green on Friday evening about sundown and arrived at Nashville on Sunday night about 2 oclock & then fell back to this place. It would be useless for me to write you concerning the fight at Fort Donnelson as the telegraph and papers will have given you all that we can learn here. A few of Greggs Regt have made their escape and are in our camp. George Dachard[35] had a brother wounded in the fight; he was left in Nashvill. Wherewe will go from here I do not know but suppose to Decater Alabama or Chattanooga. I will let you know as soon as we make our stand. Our Regiment was sent down between Nashvill & Donnelson to hunt up those that were making there escape and bring up the wagons and artillery that were left behind. They have had a hard time...no tents, nothing to eat except what they can get by chance & its raining all the time. I am looking for them in tonight. I fear several of them will be sick from being so much exposed. None of us has received a line from any of you since the 10th of January; I mean that the 10th is the latest news. I have written Nish a long letter & one to Uncle Tom and one to sister Mary since I received any. It is possible that some of the letters may have been lost in the confusion

34. James H. Hill was a younger brother who had not enlisted at this time.

35. George Decherd was from Bastrop County. He was a first sergeant in Company D of the Terry Rangers.

of things Feb. 24th. Our boys have just come in all well...John, Cap, Bob and Bud McGuire. The Yanks are in Nashville I reckon. Give my love to all enquiring friends & as soon as we get quartered again I will write you Particulars.

Bob

John W. Hill to Mary Scott Hill

Corinth Miss April 17, 1862

Miss M. S. Hill
Bastrop

Dear Sister

It has only bin a few dayes sinse I wrote to you but it is the last chance that I may have in some time and Capt Moring from our Company is going to Texas. We are now ordered to be ready to leave here day after tomorrow. All the calvary is under one Brigadier-General and it is said that we are going back to Tennesse. I do not know for what purpose. We are not going to take any wagons withe us, nothing but pack mules. Brother Tom and Company got to this place day before yesterday. Bro Tom, Geo McGehee and Sam Watkins[36] joined this Company for the war. All the rest of the Company joined a three months Company that has joined the Regment lately. Wm. Hunt has not joined any Company. Brother Bob has got back from Aburdean. He looks a greal deal better but is not well yet. He is going back down there tomorrow and stay till he gits well. He reported all well down there when he come up. Capt Ferrill is quite Sick and is going down with Bro

36. Sam Watkins was from San Marcoa.

Bob. Lieut Burdett has resigned and is going home. There has ben two discharges since we got to this place from our Company. F. T. Bots from Travis Co., King Stuard from Burlesin Co. and James McGuire took Frank down to his uncles about twenty miles below Grand Junction. I have not heard a word from them sinse they left. I am afraid that Frank is very sick as Jim only intended to stay a few dayes. Cap was very glad when Dick[37] told him that Aunty[38] had sent him a Negro to Cook. He does very well for a new hand. Scott you will see more in the papers about the fight here than I could write to you in a week. The news came a few dayes ago that Fort Pilow had fallen but the papers of 16th from Memphis did not say any thing about it. Bro Tom and Company had a pleasant trip of it. Dick Royston is gone down in Miss withe his Bro-in-law Mr. Pruit to get a horse. He has not bin Sworne in yett. Scott you must excuse all mistakes and write soon. My Love to all and axcept the same for yourselfe.

Your Bro,
John. W. Hill

I wrote to Sister Sarah some time sinse. Has she received the letter? All the boyes join me in love to you all.

37. Dick- Dick Roiston who had been home on a leave.
38. Aunty was Mrs. T. B. J. Hill, the mother of "Cap."

John W. Hill to Mary Scott Hill

Florence Co., Ala May 6 (No Year)

Miss M. S. Hill

Dear Sister

Though I have not heard from any of you sinse Dick Royston left home, I felt it my duty to write by eavry one that is going to Texas. We are now on our way up in Tenn. We will cross the River tomorrow. We will then be in the rear of all the Enemy forces that are at Corinth. We expect to have very servise when we git there. We have about thirty five hundred cavalry, three pieces of artilery. We are all well except Bro Tom; he has taken severe cold and has had some fever but is up to go. Bro Bob & Capt Farill left us whilest we were at Corinth and went down to Aberdine. I have not heard from him sinse but he was looking a great deal better when he left us the last time. Dick Royston left us whiles we were at Corinth, went down in Miss withe his Brother-in-law. [He] has not returned yet though we are looking for him every day. Scotts and Morgans Cavalry came up here ahead of us. Scotts Regment crossed the River.

Several dayes ago went up to Athens in Tenn, attacked one Regiment of Infantry and two hundred Yankees Cavalry and shipped them. They took twenty prisoners, five wagons and teams, burned a R.R. Bridge. And whilest the Bridge was on fire, there was a freight train withe 260 sacks of coffee besids a great deale of other freight. It run into the Fire and all was burned up. They took a great many gunns, ammunition and tents. Frank McGuire is still down at his Uncle's below Gra-Junction. Jim[39] sayes when he left him that he was a great deal better. You must excuse all mistakes as this is written in haste. My Love to all and axcept the same for yourselfe

Your Bro,
Jno. W. Hill

39. Jim McGuire, a brother of Frank McGuire. They were cousins of the Hills.

P. S. We have heard that they have had a big fight in Virginia, that Lee & Johnson were bothe killed on our Side, that McClellon was a prisoner and that we had gained a Glorious victory. I hope that it may prove true. All the boyes send there Love to you all. We are now camped about eight miles from Courtland near the Tennassee River. We are in a very rich country, have plenty of forage for our horses and plenty for our Selves.

T. A. HILL[40] TO JOHN W. HILL

Cumberland Gap May 19, 1862

J. W. F. Hill

Dear Cousin

You cant form no Idear of the relief your letter gave me. It is the first time I have heard from any of you since the fight of Shighlo. All is still quiet at this place. Rumor states that we will leave here in a few days for the interior of Ky led by Major General E. Kirb Smith with twenty thousand (20,000) troops. How true I don't know. Would not be surprized if it was so. A light Battery of eight guns arrived here yesterday & an immense amount of commissary stores are being collected here and the roads between here and the R.R. fixed for the transportation of Artillery and Wagon trains. I received a letter from Georgia a few days since. All were well and the prospect for a heavy crop was never more flattering. John tell Cap to take care of his Money and not spend it foolishly; that I have plenty as long as it lasts and when it gives out I will manage to get more by some means. John, to give you some Idear of how things sell here I will give you the price of a few

40. T. A. Hill was a brother of D. O. Hill. See Note 7.

articles: Chickens from $1.00 to $1.50. Turkey $2.00. Eggs 50 cts. Dryed fruit $3.00 per bushel. Butter 75 cts. So you see that it costs something for me to live here. The last letter I got from home was before Uncle Nish started. Consequently nothing later than you have heard. John, write to me frequently; I will pay all postage. I believe you are the only one of my kin belonging to the rangers that will condescend so much as to write to me. Tell all of my friends howdy.

Your Cousin,
T. A. Hill

P. S. Direct [letters] to Cumberland Gap

ROBERT E. HILL TO MARY SCOTT HILL

Camp. Ford. May 25, 1862
Near Courtland. Ala.

My Dear Sister

I know not whether this will ever reach you or not however the anxiety which you all must feel for our welfare & safety makes it a duty as well as it gives me pleasure to communicate with you. I have been for the last month very unwell so much so that I have spent the most of the time at Aberden Miss., though I have been with our company now nearly a week at this place. Brother Tom [and] Brother John are both well. Cousin Bob has been sick and is now staying at a private house in the country, 2½ miles from here & Cap is staying with him. Bob is up and about, will be able to be with us again in a few days. Bud Mcguire & Jim are both so well so is John Tom McGehee.[41] All of the friends & acquaintances,

41. Tom McGehee was a cousin of the Hills. He lived in Fayette County.

except Cousin Bob, that are here are well and getting along very well. Cousin Nish is with a party that have gone up into Tennessee. We heard from them last night. They were at Winchester, all well and in very good spirits. I do not know when we will move from here but guess we will not be here very long. The movements of the army are very uncertain now. If we whip them at Corinth Miss., we will move from here right on into Tennessee and Kentuck again. Our troops are very confident and expect to give them a warm reception at Corinth.

They have skirmish fighting nearly every day at Corinth in which we generally get the best of it. Brother John had my horse killed under him in a fight with the Yanks up on the other side of the River some two weeks ago. Our boys succeeded in taking 49 prisoners with one Capt & Lieut. Brother Tom was also in the fight. All escaped unhurt. It does seem that the Almighty has us under special protection in answer to the prayers of the loved ones at home. May he continue his divine protection untill this unnatural war shall terminate is my daily Prayer.

Your Brother,
Bob

Give my love to all.

John W. Hill to Mary Scott Hill

Chatanooga Tenn June 16, 1862

Miss. M. S. Hill
Bastrop

Dear Sister

Though it has ben nearly two months sinse I heard from you, and it may be many more before I will have the pleasure of hearing again, I feel it my duty to write to you by eavry opportunity that presents itselfe and hope that you will do the same. We are all [well.] In fact I never saw so little sickness in the Regment before. When I last wrot to you we were on our way up in Tenn. We crossed the Tennessee River near Courtland in Ala. When we got across there was ten men from several of the companys selected to go up some thirty miles to see what the Enemy was doing and what was their numbers. There was some seventy or eighty of us. We went up on the Decater & Nashvill Rail Road some thirty miles from where we crossed the river, attacked some seventy of the Enemy that was guarding a trusle work on the R.R. We killed seventeen of them and took forty-nine prisoners. They killed two privates and one Captain, a Mr Haris from Gonzales Co. They killed the horse that I was riding. They shot the strap partly that fastenes my saddle and killed my horse dead in his tracks. I do not think that the ball missed my leg by more than an inch. But whilest they were shooting I had the satisfaction of knowing that I was returning the compliment and I hope with good effect. After we went back to River the next day, Col. Whorton, the first Kentucky and about two hundred Tenn Cavalry making in all about seven or eight hundred under Brig Genl Adams, left on a two dayes scout. They left about seventy or eighty men with the wagons to cross them back across the River. I was one of the number left withe the wagons. We got the wagons back across the River about twelve o'clock the night after they left. But we thought that we would stay on the other side of the River till the

Regment got back. We went up to a little town about four miles from the River and was having our horses shod. About one o'clock our picket was run in and we learned that very soon there was about four thousand of the Enemy upon us. You ought to have seen us saddle up and git. We all got back on this side of the river by going about twenty miles below and crossing the River after night. So you will see that the Regment was cutt off from us and had to come up to this place to git back on this side. We are all together once more. Those that was cutt off had a hard time of it. All of Company D is going home when their time is out which is the last of this monthe if Mr Conscription will let them off. They are all gitting very tired of the Servise so far from home. We have very cheering news from Virginia. No fighting in Miss. sinse our army fell back from Corinthe. It is the report that Brig Genl John C. Breckneridge with his Brigade of about ten thousand men is on his way here and that we are going to operate withe him in Tenn & Kentucky. I received a letter from Cousin Tom A. Hill dated the sevnthe of this month from Cumberland Gap he says that he is in fine healthe. I wrote to him to come down and think he will iff he can git off to see his Uncle Nish and the other relations before they leave for home. He said that [he had] received some letters from Georgia and all the relations were well. Bro Bob got back to the regiment about three weeks ago from Aberdeane. He reports all well down there. Lt Col Walker has resigned and I would not be surprised iff Capt Ferrill is not elected in his place. We were all paid a few dayes ago. It is the first time I have received a cent since I have been in Service. You must write if you git a chance.

J. W. Hill

P. S. I was in town having my horse shod when I wrote the first of this. On returning to camp I found a letter from Cousin Tom which I send thinking that Uncle Tom & Aunt Scott would like to see something from him. Cap had broke it open and you can see the mark of his hand in the greasy spot that is on it. On looking at the post mark I find that is written way back in May. I received a letter up to the 7th of this monthe and would send it but have lost it. All the boyes send their love to you All.

From your Brother,
Jno. W. Hill

Crocket says tell all the folks howdey[42]

ROBERT EDWARD HILL TO MARY SCOTT HILL

June the 16, 1862
Camp Lookout. Near Chattanooga

Sister Mary

As we are intirely cut off from any mail communication with our loved ones at home we have to take every opportunity [when] we can find any one going to Texas to send by hand. And as the dark hours thicken around us, faint hearts & craven spirits come crowding on us for discharges and we have several opportunities of sending by hand. We are now encamped at the foot of Lookout Mt. waiting patiently for the Yanks to make their attack on Chattanooga. On Sunday the 8th they shelled the place but did very little damage, shooting through some houses and killing one old cow and scaring a horse so bad that he broke out the stable and ran off. No one on our side was killed and but 2 men wounded. One had 2 fingers of his left hand shot off and one of Col. Morgans men was shot in the mouth, the ball passing out through the cheek. We have had a hard trip from where we were encamped to this place. The last letter that I wrote you we were then near Courtland Alabama. From there to here it is something near 160

42. Crockett was the negro who was sent by Mrs. T. B. J. Hill to wait on the Hill boys.

miles. A portion of our regiment were cut off on the north side of Tennessee River and had to make their way through 20,000 Yankees around Huntsvill, and other places but they all got through safe & sound and we are all together at this place. They had to travel most of the time at night and had to eat just anywhere they could get. I think Cousin Nish was the worst shipped man I ever saw—near 6 weeks without any clothing except what he had on. You may guess how he looked when we got to them with the wagons. Nish has stood the trip much better than I had any idea he would stand it. I think he is improving in health, weight & strength. The company that he joined, their time is out and I guess that he will soon be on his way unless they are held by the conscript law and I imagine that with the prospect that is now open in Texas they will still be allowed to go on home and join the service there. You are all very anxious to hear from us but you know not how anxious we are to hear from home. The last news we had from home that was reliable was by Mr. Powell.[43] He found us at our Camp near Courtland and is still with us. He is not going to join but will remain with us a short time and then return back to Texas. When he gets back he can tell you a thousand things that we never think of in writing. The health of our Regt is better now than it has ever been since we first landed in Ky. Not many sick, Brother Tom & John has just got back from a three days scout down the river where they have had a good view of the Yanks on the other side of the Tennessee River. I do not know whether they will come up here and attack this place again; or whether they are attempting to make their way into East Tennessee and keeping a force on the river here to prevent our Cavalry from crossing the river; or whether they intend crossing below here and aim to go down into the into Georgia. Their movements at this time are very uncertain and ours equally as uncertain as theirs. We do not know at what moment we may be ordered from here or where we will go to when we leave here. Our life that we

43. Mr. Powell was Mr. Pomp Powell, who lived in La Grange.

are living now is right tight. Our coffee has given out so that we can get no more. And our diet now is fat, meat and sometime cornbread but most usually flour. There are more poor people just along the road that we traveled from Courtland to this place than in the whole of Texas put together. More big fat barefooted girls than I ever saw in all of my life before. I did not know that there was such a poor lot of people in the south outside of our large cities and what I regret to have to say [is that] a great many of them are still for the Glorious Union, ready & willing to give the Yankes any information of our movements. They think that the Yanks will get on this side of the river and they, by giving [the Yanks] information, will escape unhurt & unharmed. They know that we do not want to harm them & they want to make sure with the enemy. Most of them are too cowardly to do anything down in Alabama in those mountains regions. They enlisted and are now deserting and getting back home. Some of them just enlisted to get the bounty and as soon as they get it, some morning finds them on their way back home. Such men are worthless even in the army and we are better off without them than with them. They create confusion.

Brother John received a letter from Cousin Tom Ander. this morning. He is still at Cumberland Gap under Genl. Kirby Smith. Cousin Tom says with the reinforcements which are on their way there that Genl. Smith will have 20,000 men under his command. I do not know myself what he expects to do. Genl. Jackson is doing good service in Va. and the Richmond papers of the 14th say that an English fleet of 16 war vessels were off Hampton roads. Their intentions were not known. I do not give it much credit myself for I do not believe in foreign interference. I have no idea that England and France are going to get themselves mixed up in this affair since they let the Mason & Slidell affair pass off so quietly & then besides, I believe that we can win our own independence without their help. And of course if we do we can then dictate the terms of peace whereas if foreign powers interfere in this settlement it can only be a patched up compromise that will be to our disadvantages. It is true that no one wishes for this unholy & unchristian war to end more than I do but I do not want to see our Govmt. fettered by any compromise that will act [against] us in years to come.

I have said enough for this letter of movements and our hopes & fears. Now for the boys.

Brother Tom is very well and always ready & willing for any duty. Brother John is also in fine health & good spirits. Cousin Cap Hill is in good health; sings and whistles and keeps in first rate humor, stands [war] as well as any man in the company. Bob Hill was quite sick while we were encamped at Courtland but he went out to the private house of a man by the name of McGee, where there was two fat bouncing young ladies, and got well directly on strawberries & cream. Frank McGuire is fat as a pig and in fine spirits. Jim Mcguire has the yellow Jaundice and is staying at a private house in the Country. Cousin George McGehee is not very well and he is staying with Jim. I do not think either of them will be under the weather long

Cousin Nish as I have said before stands it much better than I thought he would. Gus Hill stands it very well I think he has grown since he has come and Gus says that he is at least 15 years older than when he left home. Bob Hubbard stands it very well. He has not been sick any since he left Home. Bob Price & John Jenkins are both sick now at a private House one mile from camp. Dr. John Watson stands it very well. They were all on that trip in Tennessee and were pretty well used up for a while untill they got a chance to rest awhile—I do not believe that Bob Price will be able to stand the service.

I believe that I have given you all that will interest you in our whereabouts and condition and will now ask you as a favor for all the boys in camp to read and let this be read generally to all white & black. I forgot to mention Crockett. His cane quills are as popular in camps as anything else. He is well.

The boys all join me in love to you all & whenever you can get a chance to write, do so, for you have no ideas how we want to hear from you. When any of us will get Home the Good Lord above only knows. But we all live in hopes that before another winter is through we will again be around our fireside & then we can talk of the scenes and sufferings of a soldiers life and the privations which we are now passing through. Give my love to all.

Your Brother,
Bob

John W. Hill to Mary Scott Hill

Bards-town Ky, Sept 26, 1862

Miss. W. S. Hill

Dear Sister

As Mr. Shouler is going to start home in the morning I fell that it is my duty to write to you. Though I feel very little like wrighting for I have just come off of a long and hard scout sinse we crossed the Tenasse River at Chattanooga on the 3rd of July. We have not had in all over five dayes rest, traveling many times all day and knight and many times without anything to eat. On the 18th of this monthe our Briggad moved withe Major General Polk's division of the army in the rear of about five thousand of the Enemy at Woodsenville the place that Col Terry was killed at last fall. Whilst General Buckner engaged them on the other side of Green River where we come upon them in the rear they surrendered without firing a gun. We took over five-thousand prisoners, eleven piece of artillery and an emmence amount of army stores. Two dayes after the capture of this force it was reported that General Buell was advancing upon General Bragg from Bowling-Green. So you will see by this that General Bragg had managed to get in his rear. General Bragg commenced a retreat towards Louisville Ky.

Genl Forests & wheelers Brigades of cavalrey was left to cover his retreat on the 20th. Buells advance come up to Woodsenville and we fought them on the same ground that we had one year and one monthe before. We repulsed their Cavalrey and part of their Infantrey but they soon brought their Infantrey up in such numbers that we were obliged to fall back across the river where we gave them another round, but we were bound to fall back. We had another fight withe them the next day. We can whip any amount of cavalrey but you know that cavalrey cannot fight Infantry & artillery and that [against] vastly superior numbers we lost very few men. None out of our company. We are now camped ten miles from Bardstown on Louisville pike. Our wagons has been here several dayes but those of us that have been behind got in this morning. There was only thirty of our Company left behind. Bro Tom, Cap, F & J McGuire came on withe the wagons. Bro Tom is gone on a scout up towards Louisville. All of Genl Braggs force is here. It is said that he is going to forme a Junction withe Kirby Smith up about Lexington Ky. Nat Rives informes me that Mr. Shouler is going to start in a few minutes. I must close by saying that we are all well and in fine spirits. All send their love to you all.

Your Bro,
Jno. W. Hill

P. S. Col Whorton is Brigd General of this Brigade. Genl Forest is ordered back [to] Tenesse. Give my love to all and axcept a good portion for yourselfe.

Your Bro,
Jno W Hill

John W. Hill to Mary Scott Hill

Knoxville, Oct 26, 1862

Miss Mary S. Hill

Dear Sister

Here I sit in a cold tent withe my hands so cold that I can hardly write for the ground is white withe snow. Trying to write though it has been nearly four monthes sinse we have had a word from home. When I wrote last we were at Bardstown Ky. Sinse that time we have had a very hard time of it. We have been covering the retreat of Genl Bragg from Kentucky. At Bardstown the yanks tryed to cut us off and come very nigh doing it. They got in behind us withe a considerable cavalrey force and come very nigh gitting in their Infantry & Artilerey. Capt Jormans Company and ours was in the advance and when we pitched into them you ought to have seen them git. We took one Major, one Capitan two Lieutenants and thirty six privates. We killed some twenty or thirty. We had one man killed and two or three wounded. Brother Bob was left there with the wounded and has not come up yet. At Perryvill our Infantrey had a fight withe the advance of Buell and whipped them on the 8th of this monthe. We lost 2,500 or 3,000 whilest the Enemy lost 8,000 but they tryed to flank us and we had to fall back. I have been in many fights, but the fight at Perryvill while it lasted was the hardest I have ever seen. We lost sevral out of our Regment. Capt Evans from Gonzales was very severely wounded. We did not lose any out of our Company. Two dayes after the fight I saw Cousin Tom A. Hill. He was near Harodesburg with his comand under Kirby Smithe. He is a Lieutenant. He was in fine healthe & spirits. He was not in the fight at Perryville. I was not with him but a very short time. I guess that he will take up winter quarters about Cumberland Gap again this winter. Our waggons come on ahead of us across the mountains and we had to go several dayes without anything to eat. And we had a fight nearly every day. We arrived at this place yesterday and it is reported that we will start in a few dayes to Middle Tennasee but I do not know what field is before us. Bro Tom has been very unwell for some time but is very well at present. Cap, Bob, James & F. McGuire, Sam & Jim Watkins[44] and Geo McGehee[45] are all in fine healthe. Capitan Ferille has just come in to camp. It is the first time we have seen him sinse we left Sulpher Springs. He is looking very well and I hope that he will be able to stay withe us from this on. James P. Watkins received a letter a few dayes ago from James Thompson. He wrote that John McGehee and all of the other boyes were well. The Bush Whackers[46] give it to our wagons as they come across the mountains...[*This portion of the manuscript letter was damaged & not transcribed*] ...we come across and say that he got away but I think if he did it was at the end of a rope. I do not think that we mayd much by our trip into Kentucky. True we brought off a great deal of provisions and clothing and took a great many more prisoners than we lost but I do not think that we got more than four or five thousand recruits whilest in Kentucky.

Oct 27th—It snowed all knight last knight and as we have no tents. Cap & I had to sleep under some rails set up against a tree withe an oile clothe over them which was not very pleasant. We will get some tents today, also some clothing. Cap received a letter this morning from uncle Tom dated Sept 25th giving us the first news we have had from home sinse the first of July. You can guess with what pleasure it was read by all of us...[*This portion of the manuscript letter was damaged & not transcribed*]

I send a letter written by Bro Bob whilest we were at Bardstown Ky. I found it in his Saddle Bag. Write soon and a long letter.

O.d. Sgt. Jno W. Hill

---

44. Sam and Jim Watkins were from Hates County. They were members of Company D of the Terry Rangers.
45. George McGehee was from Hayes County. He was a cousin of the Hills.
46. "Bush Whackers" was the name often given to men who deserted or failed to join the army. The term was sometimes applied to men whose term of enlistment had expired, and they had failed to re-enlist.

John W. Hill to Mary Scott Hill

Nolensville, Williamson Co Tenn. Nov 25, 1862

Miss. M. S. Hill

Dear Sister

Your letter by Maj Shipp was received a few dayes ago whilest we were camped at Mufreysborough. We were all very glad to see Tom Gill[47] & M. Shipp once more and to hear from you all once more. I also received a letter from sister Sarah by them which is the second letter I have had from her. We left Kingston on the 8th of this month got across the mountains to Sparter on the 10th and camped there till the 18th when we left for Mufreysborough. Got there the 21st and got to this place to-day, nothing having transpired worthy of note on the road. General John Breckinridg is at Mufreysbourough with some ten or fifteen thousand troops. The rest of our troops is down towards Winchester Tenn. We are now in sixteen miles of Nashville, about nine miles of the Yankeys, and I expect that we will be after kicking up a muss withe them in a few dayes. Col Whorton is now a Brgd. General and he has some four or five thousand men under him. Col Wheeler & John Morgan are also Brgd. Generals. Whorton & Wheeler have charge of all the Cavalrey under Bragg and Morgan of all that belongs to Kirby Smiths Division.

The pen is so bad that I will try a pencil in a while. Brother Bob has got back all right and in fine healthe. The man that he was left with at Bardstown died and he went over to Perysville and stayed with our wounded of over there. He says that he cut off two mens legs whilest he was there and that they were bothe doing well when he left them. He says that the yanks acknowledge the loss of six thousand men at the battle of Perysville and that they say that it was a very shameful affare upon their part. The yanks are making the men of Kentucky take an oathe to support the Lincoln Administration. Many of the Negroes that the yank

47. Tom Gill was from Bastrop County.

soldiers stole whilest they were in Tenn were sold in Ky. Some of the children [taken] from the mothers for a quart of milk or whiskey and some ten or twelve year old boys sold for ten or twelve dollars. Brother Bob says that the yankeys treated him very well whilest he was withe them. He says that at the battle of Perrysvill that some of their new troops run clear back to Springfield. Our loss was not over twenty five hundred. They also say that we whipped them at Bardstown. The news has just come into camps that Morgan had a fight today withe the yanks between Lebanon & Mufreyabourough and that he killed two hundred and took eight hundred prisoners but I cannot vouch for the truthe of the report, though it is more than probable that it is true for John Morgan is near Lebanon and so is the Enemy, and he is the man that will fight them. Wheeler is on the pike from Murfreysbourough & Nashville whilest Whorton guards the pike from Nashville to Shelbyville. I wrote to you from Knoxville and to Sister Matt from Kingston giving you an account of our trip into Ky and as there has been nothing of interest come to pass sinse we got back into Tenn. I have nothing to write about. I want you to write longer letters. This way you have of writing one and two pages won't do. You can say to Uncle Tom that if Sister Sally[48] wants Amand[49] next year to let her keep her. And as to Wilson, [Uncle Tom] can make whatever disposition of him that he likes to do withe him as he would withe one of his own. Tell him that I would write to him but Bro Tom, Bob and Capp have all written to him and that I suppose they have given him all the news. You must excuse all mistakes and write soon and don't forget to write a long letter. All the boyes joine me in love to you all.

Your Bro,
Jno. W. Hill
O.D. Sgt. Co. D, 8th Texas Cavalrey

48. Sister Sally was the wife of T. A. W. Hill who was a brother of Bob and John Hill. He was also a member of Terry's Texas Rangers.
49. Amand and Wilson were two slaves owned by John Hill.

Robert Hill to Mary Scott Hill

Head Quarters Texas Rangers
Camp near Nolensvill Dec 8, 1862

My Dear Sister.

I wrote a few days ago to Uncle Tom by Mr. N. J. Allen and now I begin this to you & I know not whether it will ever get to its destination or not. Still it is a pleasure for me to write when ever I have an opportunity. We are still near Nashville and I judge before this reaches you a severe battle will have been fought near or at Nashville. We have an army here that is anxious to meet the Yanks & I would not be surprised at any time to hear the beginning of a big fight. We hear the booming of the cannon every day even now & have ever since my letter to Uncle Tom. The Yanks come out and shell our pickets. One half of our Regt is on picket at a time as we have several roads to watch. Our company is out now, and will stand two days. None of our boys have been hurt since I last wrote & all are well. Brother Tom started yesterday across the mountain to bring me some horses that were left over near Knoxville. He will be [absent] about some two weeks I suppose, if not longer. Jim McGuire was detailed a few days ago to go with a scouting party and has not yet returned. The boys are all well and in very good spirits. We have had a very cold spell for the last four days and even now the ground is covered with snow and everything is perfectly white. It is still very cold this morning but the sun is shining very bright and bids fair to be beautiful weather. I fear we are going to have a very cold winter and if we do, unless our army goes into Winter Quarters, there will be a great deal of suffering among the infantry as boots & blankets are very scarce & hard to get.

Genrl. Joseph E. Johnston has arrived at Murfreesburo to take command of the army that is here & the Army are moving on towards Nashvill in three columns. I can't tell whether we will attack Nashvill or whether the Yanks will give us a fight this side.

The Yanks have a force about 6 miles this side of Nashvill. Our pickets fight nearly every day.

We are getting plenty to eat and plenty for our horses. The people are anxious for our Troops to get all the surplus food of every kind as they fear that we may have to leave here again like we did last winter when the waters got up, & they know that the Yanks will take everything that they have leaving them little or nothing. The Yanks are burning up all the vacant houses wherever they go.

From the Yankees papers that we get here, I think that the army will go into Winter Quarters in Va. and the fighting, if any is done, will be done here in the west.

The French Minister is urging upon the Minister of England & Russia the necessity of making a proposition for an armistice of 6 months in which hostilities of every kind shall cease on land and sea. I hope it may be made and that a ceasation of hostilities may be brought about and then there would be some chance for peace.

And now I would like to say a few words to say to the negroes. While I was with the Yanks in Ky. I saw them selling the negro children from their Mothers for a quart of whisky and negro boys 16, 18 & 20 years old for $10 to $25. These were negroes that they had persuaded to leave their homes to be made free & that was the way they would treat them. I saw 3 or 4 men quarreling about a negro boy likely about 16 years old and they could not agree as to who had the best right to him and to end the dispute they shot the negro and killed him. The Negroes that they have taken from here are anxious to get back once more & they say they have seen enough of Yankee freedom. Crockett has seen some negroes who had been with the Yankees and who had left them and come back home. He is afraid almost to go out of camp and says that he never intends that they shall get him, that he wants to get back home again, although he is very well satisfied in camp and does not want to go home untill we all go back together. There is a general impression pervading the people here that the War will cease with the Winter or at least with next springs campaigns.

God Grant that it may last no longer then this winter and that next spring may see us all at home together.

I tried very hard to get Brother Tom a furlough to come home but it was no good. None but sick & wounded men are furloughed now. N. J. Allen got his furlough on account of family sickness.

You all must keep up a good heart at home and pray for our safety & success and our speedy return home. I believe that Our Almighty Father will hear & answer your prayers. Such is my faith in Prayer. I received a letter from Uncle Tom after I had returned from Ky., the first that I had received for 4 months. Tell Sister Sallie that I received her letter and was very glad indeed to hear from her. You can say to her that Brother Tom is in fine health and the next time she writes that she must date her letter so that we may know what time it takes to get here. Tell Cousin Nish that I have been expecting letters from him but have begun to think that he has forgotten how glad it makes a man feel in camp to get a letter from home. I am sure if I were at home that I would write every week to some of the boys here in camp, if I could only say that all were well or write who were sick, grunting or complaining. But a good warm room & good fire to sit by and a good bed to sleep in are very different from having little or no fire & snow on the ground 21 inches deep and one blanket to sleep on & about 2 to cover with, yet we must be satisfied & not grumble for we know that our young Confederacy has not grown to manhood in the way of furnishing half a million of men with every convenience. The ladies, God bless them, are knitting gloves & making socks for the soldiers all through this country and furnishing them with everything they can spare. Some of the ladies in this section have been in the habit of going into Nashvill & bringing out such things as the boys needed. One lady not longer than yesterday wore out 3 woolen over shirts under her dress & two pairs of boots & 3 hats. What a great institution hoops are.

Tell Uncle Tom & Aunt Scott that we expected to have the pleasure of Cousin Tom Anderson, as a large part of Genl Kirby Smiths army are here but Cousin Tom was in Genl. Heaths Division and he has been left in command at Knoxvill and Cumberland Gap. I suppose that Cousin Tom is still with him as we have heard nothing from him since. Cousin Tom was very anxious to come down here, I know, from what the boys all told me. John & Cap saw Cousin Tom several times in Ky and after they got to the Gap. Billy Sayers[50] has been made the Adgt. of our Regt and John Claiborn[51] is now Sgt. Major. Old Steph Ferrill is Lt. Col. and Capt Rayborn a Major. Tell Cousin Nish that Harrison as Col. steps as short as ever and holds his head so straight that it leans over behind. I believe that he is more unpopular than ever.

Our Regt is in high favor at Headquarters and they are making us do hard duty, and keeping us on the outposts all the time. We have had no rest in low these many days. We look to a grateful people at home for our reward in knowing that we have their sympathies while we are battling for all that makes life worth a cent. Our Texas troops are everywhere praised for their gallant conduct and their deeds of personal daring. I saw & talked to old United States Officers who could not be made to believe that our men were not all drunk, so close and brave did we fight them. Genl Polk issued a general order to the army in praise of our Regt. which I suppose you may have seen as several copies have been sent home & to the Editor of the *Telegraph*.

Two of our company were taken prisoners in Ky. One of them, A. T. Logan,[52] got back to camp last evening. Charlie Pelham[53] is at the Parole camp at Chattanooga. They will soon be exchanged and then come back to their company. They will have an account to settle with the Yanks as they were treated very badly by them.

The yanks are insulting the women where ever they go & threatening to burn their houses down over their heads & taking every-

---

50. Billy Sayers was from Bastrop County, Texas. His family lived in Hill's Prairie.

51. John Claiborn was from Travis County.

52. A. T. Logan was from Travis County.

53. Charlie Pelham was from Travis County. He was killed near Cleveland, Tennessee, May 9, 1864.

thing in the place that they can carry off, or destroying it some way. They are really devastating the country where ever they go. I do hope & pray that out loved land may never witness the scenes that are transpiring in this County and in Ky.

And now a few words of comfort to you all at home—Let not your hearts be troubled because of us. We have plenty to eat and are all in good health, and our hopes undimmed of the future independence of Our Young Confederacy. We yet live in hopes of getting home again where we can talk over the scenes & trials through which we have passed.

Give Our love to all enquiring friends and persuade some of them to write if you can. If you only knew how much we rejoice with each other when one gets a letter from home I know you would write oftener. There is a mail communication now running clear through and it makes no difference where we are they will send the letters to the nearest point.

Direct to "Texas Rangers" "Genl. Whartons Brigade" and they will find us.

May next spring & summer find us all together around the family circle without the loss of one either at home or here. That is the constant wish & prayer for your Brother Bob.

Goodbye. God bless & keep you as the apple of His eye.

Bob

JOHN W. HILL TO MR. J. S. POWELL[54]

Camp near Nolansville Tenn., Dec. 10, 1862

Mr. J. S. Powell

Dear Sir.

I have thought several times that I would write to you and Itasca[55] but as there was so many here from old Fayette and, as I have had so many others to correspond withe, I have put off writing till the present. Do not think hard of me for not writing to you sooner for I can assure you that here is no one for [whom] I have higher regards than for you and yours. And often do I reflect and bring back the many happy hours spent withe you as the happiest of my life. We that is the Regiment is now picketing & scouting all the time in the direction of Nashville. There is hardly a day passes but we exchange shots withe them without much damage being done to either side. Every indication is that we will have a fight here very soon. General Joseph Johnson is at Murfresboro and is [in] command of all the forces of this department. Genl Hardee is on this pike from Shelbyville to Nashville. Kirby Smithe is at Manchester and is coming in on the Lebanon pike. Generals Breckinridge, Chestom & Withors are on the pike from Murfresboro to Nashville. Brigd Genl John H. Morgan had a fight at Huntsville a few dayes ago and killed some five hundred, took eighteen hundred or two thousand prisoners, about sixty waggons and four pieces of artillery, a considerable amount of arms and ammunition. Genal Rosencranz is in command of the federal forces at Nashville. Genl Buell has been removed and was brought into Nashville under guard. He was brought there to stand his trial before a Court Marshal for treason. We get

54. Mr. J. S. Powell was from La Grange. He owned a mercantile store where John Hill was clerking when the Civil War began.

55. Itasca was the wife of Mr. Powell. She was the niece of Mrs. T. B. J. Hill, and was reared by "Aunty and Uncle."

Nashville & Louisville papers every few dayes. There is several ladies from this country that go into Nashville every few dayes. And one Lady a few dayes sinse wore out three overshirts, several pairs Boots, hats etc. What a great thing hoops are. Some of them have brought out several blankets, Six Shooters and several suits of Confederate Grey all under them...We have a paper here containing Old Abe's Message. He urges his emancipation policy. I will send you a copy of the paper if I can get one. I see from Northern papers that they are fitting up an Expadition under Genl Banks to send to Texas. Some of the Northern Papers are opposed to his being sent to Texas and say that he ought to be attached to Burnsides to march upon Richmond. The Yanks are making grand preparations to march upon us as soon as the Rivers git up so as there Iron Clad Boats can move but by the help of God and Minny Balls we met them and turned their course once, and I hope and believe that we will do it again. But withe all of our success when we look at our dessimated ranks and think of this Regt. when it left Texas with over one thousand noble Spirits and now in it we only have some Four or five hundred, and think of the noble fellows that have fallen, some upon the bloodey field, some by disease it makes our hearts sad. We have no late news from Virginia. The last was Burnsides had demanded the surrender of Fredtratsburg and that Lee and refused to give it up. Major Harison is now Col. of this Regt. Capt S. C. Ferill is Lt. Col. & Capt Rubon is Major. Capt Jormon is on the sick list. He has been quite unwell for some time but has been upgoing within the last few dayes. Dick Jormon wase paroled whilest we were in Ky and has not been exchanged as yet. Major Thornton and Drisdal that were wounded at the Stockage fight last August have got well and returned to their Company. All the boyes of Capt Jormons Company are well. Nat is in fine health and went withe his company this morning on picket. We had two men caught and paroled out of our Company whilest we were in Ky, A. T. Logan & Charley Pelham. They are bothe from Travis Co. and I do not know that you know them. Dr. T. J. Potts[56] of our Company was appointed Surgon of the Regt by Col. Whorton whilest we were at Corinthe. He went up to Mufreysburo a few days ago to stand his Examination before the Medical Board and failed. They wrote him a note stating that his Examination was not satisfactory and that his resignation would be received. He came back and fixed up his tricks and left for parts unknown without saying a word to but one or two about it. He met our Company in the road as he was leaving and never said a word to them. Bro Tom has gone over the Mountains to Kingston after some Horses that we left over there to recruit up and will be gone for some ten or fifteen dayes. Bro Bob is in fine healthe so is Cap & Bob Hill; in fact all the boyes of your acquaintance. You must remember me to all my old friends around La Grange. My love to Cousin Lizzie and Itasca[57]and except the same for yourselfe. Excuse all mistakes and wrote soon and a long letter.

Yours Truly,
Jno. W. Hill
O. D. Sgt Company D
8th Texas Cavalry

I got Lt. Decherd to back this as he was using the pen & ink and he has franked it. I will let it go as I have no stamp.

56. T. J. Potts was born in England, but his home at this time was in Bastrop County.

57. Cousin Lizzie was Lizzie Yates, and Itasca was Itasca Powell. They were reared by Mrs. T. B. J. Hill.

Robert Edward Hill to Mary Scott Hill

Hd. Quarters, Tex. Rangers
Camp near Shelbyville, Jan. 12, 1863

My Dear Sister,

I would have written to you sooner, but have been absent from any of our boys that you know and with some who were wounded in the fight which took place at Murfresboro which you will have heard of long before this reaches you. Our Regiment was in that fight and we lost in killed, wounded & Missing about 70 men. Brother John is in the hands of the Enemy. His horse was shot from under him and Capt. Ferg Kyle tried to get Brother John up behind him but the Yanks were so close on him that Brother John told him to save himself and he would have to surrender. Several of the regiment saw Brother John get back to the wagons of the Enemy & I feel very sure that he was not wounded unless they did it when he surrendered. If he is not wounded he will be exchanged very soon and will again be with us. Our Brigade got into the rear of the Enemy and were destroying their wagon train and taking prisoners when [they] sent a force back to attack us that was too much for us. We had to give back and in giving back after we had destroyed a good many of their wagons was when they got Brother John. They also had me for nearly two days but I had no chance to see Brother John and, in fact, did not know that they had Brother untill I saw the Comp after the fight was over. We had several wounded and I stooped to dress their wounds and before I was through I was in the Yankes lines. I got all our Reg. that was with me out but one. You can tell Cousin Nish that Phil Mullen[58] was wounded in the leg (not broke.) Wayne Hamilton[59] also. Both belonged to our Comp. They were the only ones wounded at Murfresboro (I forgot to mention K. K. Rector.) J. P.

---

58. Phil Mullen was from Burleson County.
59. Wayne Hamilton was from Travis County.

Billingsley & Dave Nunn[60] were both wounded before the fight at Murfresboro and while we were fighting them from Nolensville. Billingsley was wounded on Christmas day. They were both doing well the last time I saw him, both able to ride on horseback. Cousin Cap, Bob Hill, Brother Tom, Cousin Jim & Frank McGuire, Cousin George Mcgehee are all doing very well and safe thus far. Have we not reason to be grateful to Our Heavenly Father for his protection & merciful kindness in our preservation while so many have fallen on [both] sides. The fight at Murfresboro is one of the hardest fought Battles and I suppose the heaviest loss on each side since this war began. I have heard that our loss was between 7 & 8,000 killed & wounded. The Yanks admit a loss so says Genrl. Cheatham of 25,000. We took some where near 7,000 prisoners and had their army as I thought completely whipped on Wednesday and I believe now if Genrl. Bragg had crowded the center & left wing as we did on the left we would have had a complete rout. We drove their right wing at least 3 miles strewing the woods with dead & wounded Yankees. But from some cause I know not what, our left wing was stopped and the fight was kept up with cannon untill after dark. The next day the Armies lay in front of each other maneuvering and nothing was done except skirmishing. So passed Thursday. On Friday the same thing untill about 3 o'clock p.m. when General Breckinridge pushed his column on and drove the Enemy about a mile when they rallied their forces and retook the ground over which Breckenridge had driven them. We all expected that Saturday would open the ball anew but to our surprise nothing of the kind took place and Saturday night our forces were withdrawn from the field that they had held in front of a force stated to be greatly their superior in number. We buried our dead and brought off our wounded and are now here. What will be done next I am not able to say. The Enemy occupies Murfresboro and have their pickets out five miles this side and our Reg as usual is right in their face. This place Shelbyvill is 25

60. K. K. Rector, J. P. Billingsley and Dave Nunn were all from Bastrop County.

miles from Murfresboro. If the Enemy are not satisfied with our acquaintance at Murfresboro and follow us up, I expect we will give them another turn here. It will be some time before he can move as we destroyed his wagon train or at least between 4 & 500 wagons and all the mules to the wagons and supplies in the wagons. He will have to refit before he can try again. I hardly think he will follow us. You can tell Cousin Nish that Paul Jim Watkins[61] is also a prisoner. He was left at a Yankee Hospital to see that the surgeons were not interfered with by order of General Wharton, and when our force's cavalry fell back Jim was left and the Yanks got [him.] One of the Surgeons said to our boys that he knew me at Perryville and that he would see that Paul, Jim & Brother John should want for nothing. I made the acquaintance of some of the Yankee surgeons in Ky that were very clever and perfect Gentlemen. By Genl Wharton having them treated kindly while he had them, they may take notice & see that Brother John, Paul and Jim are properly treated and furnish them with whatever they may need. At least I hope so.

Sam Fredberger[62] was wounded on the day before the fight by our own infantry. Sam acted hastily and was very much in the wrong or he would not have been shot. Genl. Wharton was sent out of Tuesday to find out their position and was told that the Enemy were flanking him on the left so he extended his line and sent back word to Lt. General Polk who sent a brigade of Infantry and a battery of Artillery to protect a road. Sam was sent out on the left and came upon our infantry skirmishers and they ordered him to halt where he was. Soon as he saw them, supposed they were Yankees, drew his pistol and fired, hitting the man that he fired at. They turned loose upon him, hitting him in two places a flesh wound in the side [and] a very serious wound in the hip. I saw him on Friday, 4 days after the wound. I very much fear that

61. Paul Jim Watkins was from Hayes County. He was wounded at Greensborough, Georgia in 1864.
62. Same Fredberger was from Bastrop County.

he will die as he had Erysipelas. I left him in Murfresboro. K. K. Rector was wounded through the arm and was put in an ambulance and they boys were not able to bring him off, so the Enemy has got him. Bob Shipp has been missing ever since the 26th. We suppose the Enemy has got him & Joe Ford[63] as they were together the last that was seen of them.

We have had a good deal of rain putting the streams all up which I suppose was the reason of our backward movement as our Battle line extended diagonally across Stone River there at Murfresboro. A part of our force were on one side and a part on the other and to have drawn them all on this side would have to place us this side of Murfresboro 5 miles. There the Duck River at this place would still be in our rear and I suppose Genrl. Bragg deemed it prudent to get on Duck River.

I cannot but yet think that the fight that is to end this war will be fought in Missippi— and the next fight that will be made will be in Missippi if one is not already begun there.

I do hope that this war will cease this next spring and that we may weather the storm, ride safely out and all meet again around our fireside when we can enjoy each others society without the fear of Yanks or anyone else to trouble us.

And now My Dear Sister I know not hardly how to express myself or how to give consolation to our Dear Mother. I miss Brother John and no longer hear his cheerfull voice for he was nearly always trying to sing some song or had so much to say. I miss him so much yet I feel sure that he was not wounded and thankful to our Heavenly Father that he was not killed and is only a prisoner. Yet, I know, from Brother John's nature that it is almost death for him to be a prisoner and in their hands, and I hope that it will not be long before he is exchanged and will be again with us. You must try and bear it with as much fortitude as you can summon to your support, and trusting to Our Heavenly Father to take care of him while he is in the hands of the Enemy.

---

63. Joe Ford was from Bastrop County.

Tell Sister Sallie that Brother Tom was absent when I received her last letter to him & I broke it open & read it and have not seen him untill today to have any chance to talk with him. I gave him her letter to read and he says that he has just closed one to her and, as to moving home, she must do as she thinks best as he is here and she there. She must act as she thinks best for the future.

January 13th—We have just moved our camp. We are now camped with the Wagon train between Murfresboro & Shelbyvill some 21½ miles from Shelbyvill. I expect that our regiment will come to the wagons and do as we did at Nolensvill—one half of the Regiment do duty at a time. The Enemy are still at it & just this side of Murfresboro have thrown up breastworks to protect themselves from our cavalry. We have just heard of the recapture of Galveston & we feel proud of Texas & the Texas troops. Our Regiment & the Brigade of Texas under Genl Ector did the hardest fighting that was done at Murfresboro & we took as many prisoners as the rest of the Entire army. All Honor to Texas.

And now My Dear Sister you must continue to ask our Heavenly Father to continue his blessing and protection over us that he may save us from the hands of the Enemy & return us safely at home.

Give my love to all enquiring friends and accept a large share for yourself. Crockett says tell them all howdy for him and to Liza[64] that he does not intend for the Yanks to get him, as he wants to get back to see her. He thinks of her every day and dreams of her at night. My love to all. Say to Scott that Cap is a good Boy.

Bob

---

64. Liza was a slaved owned by the Hills.

Robert Edward Hill to Mary Scott Hill

January the 14, 1863

My Dear Sister

A Gentleman belonging to the 2nd Georgia made his escape after being carried to Nashvill and says that he saw one of our Regt. in Nashvill by the name of Griffin, and that Griffin told him that Brother John with several others were in the Penetentiary at Nashvill. Griffin was taken prisoner several days before Brother John was taken. I feel very sure that John will be with us as soon as they can take him to Louisville and down to Vicksburg where they [keep] prisoners. I hope that close confinement will not make him sick. Capt. Kyle says that he feels that he must write to Ma telling her that he has done everything that he could do to save Brother. He stayed with him trying to get John up behind him untill the Yankees were in thirty yards of him and John told him to save himself.

Capt Kyle can hardly keep from crying when anything is said. He says that John was the Flower of the Comp and if it could have been so he would have rather lost any one else than John—always ready for duty, ever willing, John had won the good opinion of all who knew him and had won the esteem of all the officers in the regiment.

You must tell Mrs. Shipp when you see her or any of the family that Bob Shipp is missing. I feel very sure that he is not wounded and will be with us again as soon as an exchange can be effected.

Tell Cousin Nish he can say to Mr. Rector that K. K. Rector was wounded through the arm, the boys say in two places, and they think that the bone was broke. He was very sick from the wound and they put him in an ambulance that had been captured but was compelled to leave him in the hands of the Enemy. If I had known it when I was with them I would have gone to see him but of course I knew not who were wounded except those that I would work on untill after I got back to the Comp. Our Regt is just going on outpost duty again. The Enemy show no signs yet of advancing. Write soon & often. Give my love to all enquiring friends and accept a share youself.

Your Brother,
Bob

Author Unknown[65] to Mary Scott Hill

Headquarters Texas Rangers
Near Louisberg, Tenn., Feb 18, 1863

Miss Scottie Hill

Dear Miss:

Your welcomed letter reach me yesterday of Dec. 13th. I was highly pleased to learn that you all were well although I must acknowledge that I was disappointed in the length of your letter. I expected a long letter from you. Your first has not come to hand yet. When you write you ought to remember the Golden Rule "Do unto others as you would have them to do unto you." That is to say, write long letters and if I fail to do the same, then shock my memory. We have a great deal to write about sometimes, but have not pen, ink, or paper. If we would get those things, we would write oftener. We are not situated like you all. When we write, we have to write on a book or a piece of barrel head. You all write on a table, which is a decided advantage to one, so far as comfort is concerned. Enough on that subject.

Now for the news. On the 28th of Jan. we left Shelbyville on a big scout. The morning before we left Shelbyville it snowed until

65. This letter was likely written by Oliver or Bob Ship.

the snow was three or four inches on the ground. We left on the 28th in the morning, and travelled that day 18 or 20 miles and camped in the snow. Some of us got hey and others got fodder to make our bed down upon. In that way we rested very comfortably that night. Our company was on Picket that we far[ed] very well. At daylight the next morning, the 29th we were on the line of march. We knew not where we were bound for. We travelled all that day and until about 3 o'clock. We reached Franklin and there we camped until 12 o'clock the next day. At 12 o'clock we left Franklin, for Sharlotsville but we did not go to Sharlotsville that day and we camp this side of it. The next day we reached Sharlotsville and stopped there awhile on some business. From there we had to go twenty miles to camp on account of forage. The next morning we were as usual on our march. We travelled until 3 o'clock, and built up fires to warm by. While we were standing by the fires, we heard two cannons at Fort Donelson after which we were ordered to mount out horses (all this time, we did not know where we was going to. Some thought Fort Donelson, and others to different points.) We had not gone far, before some of the boys enquired how far it was to Fort Donelson, and to our surprise we were in three miles of F. D., our gait keeping faster and faster until we got to the fort. Our Regiment, very near the rear, as soon as we got in sight of the Fort the Brigade was halted, and the Rangers ordered to the front. I thought we had to go into the fight, in the advance, as we always have done before, but to my surprise the Rangers were ordered on the road leading from F. D. to Fort Henry. That was on the extreme left wing of our line of Battle. We had about five thousand cavalrymen, no Infantry, about fifteen piece of artillery. Gen. Wheeler was in command. There was Gens. Forrester & Wharton's Brigades of Cavalry. We fought them three hours, driving them from breastworks to breastworks, finally into the fort. In the fight we lost a great many. They had the advantage of us in position. Our batteries in fight killed very near all of their horses in their batteries. They dismounted one cannon, & the 2nd Georgia Regiment was dismounted and fought as Infantry. They fought bravely; they captured a cannon and brought it out. They deserve a great deal of credit for bravery on that occasion. We fought until dark, when we fell back under the cover the trees. Our boys had not been there [long] before four Gunboats came to the rescue of the Fort. They brought with them, several transports with reinforcements. We did not wait to see how [many] for the gunboats commenced shelling us as soon as they got there. We fell back two miles, and camped that night. Next morning we took up a line of march to this place. Both going and coming, we were in snow all the time. Our feet while riding would freeze to our stirrups. We had to get down off our horses and walk to keep from freezing. A good many of the boys had their toes frost bitten. In the long run I think we will loose more then we gained. We captured about fifty prisoners; with them we got forty negroes. Our Regiment did no fighting that day. Consequently we didn't lose a single man. After the fight we marched in snow all the way back until we got to Columbia. There we camped two or three days and then came to this place, where we are at present in mud up to our knees. We would have taken Fort Donelson but our ammunition gave out, both for the small arms and artillery, and we had to fall back. Some of our Regiments didn't have a single round in there cartridge boxes. There was several other little occurrences, too numerous to mention. We are not at the wagons. We will, I expect, go on another wildgoose chase before long. I have no late news to mention this writing. The newspapers are filled with good news, if it can only be so. In the Winchester papers, the late telegraphic news is the that Louis Napoleon has offered mediation, bothe to North & South; Indiana, Illinois, Ohio and Kentucky are to meet (I mean their commissioners) in Frankfort today to form a Western Confedracy and also to send commissioners to Richmond Va. to bring about Peace! Their papers are asking for Peace, the main Abolition leaders in the North are calling for Peace & they can't— [*Letter ends abruptly*]

ROBERT EDWARD HILL TO MARY SCOTT HILL

Hd. Qtrs 8th Texas Rangers
Camp Berling Tennessee, Feb 23, 1863

My Dear Sister

I would have written to you before this but that I had written to Uncle Tom & to Cousin Nish and also to little Cousin Alice & I knew that you would get to see them. In fact when I write to one then I write to all and when we get a letter here it is like all of us getting one. So you see why I do not write to any one of you so often. I write every two weeks almost regular to someone there at home & I expect to keep it up as long as the war lasts or as long as there are any chances to get letters through. If Cap & Tom & the other boys were to write as often as I do you would get letters oftener than you do. Brother John wrote regular untill he was taken by the Yankees at Murfresboro. I have not heard from him as yet. K. K. Rector has come in. He made his escape from them and is now getting out his papers for Discharge as his arm was broke and he will no longer be fit for service. I will send this by him. I hope you may get to see him. He can tell you a great deal of our wanderings and our fights and give you a good deal of information that you may want to know and which I might never think about writing.

My Dear Sister I received your letter that you wrote to John. It gave me great pleasure to read it I assure you. I do wish you would write every week. I know I would if I had some place where we could stay but we have to move almost every week, never staying at a place long enough to get anything fixed. When we do stay it is at this season of year, either raining, sleeting or snowing, so that we can have no comfort in anything or pleasure either except when we get letters from home. Then we forget everything in the pleasure it affords us in reading yours & writing in answer. I have not received a letter from you directed to myself in I don't know when, yet I believe that you have written and that the letters have been miscarried. You can't tell how proud we were to receive things you all sent us. Anything from home makes us feel glad all over. Then for us to know that while we are undergoing hardships & trials in the Field our loved ones at home are thinking of us & are doing all that they possible can do for our comfort, it makes our hearts glad & cheers us on to Double Duty. The Texas Rangers feel proud of the Women of Texas and we live in hopes that it will not be long before we get back to share your smiles and affections.

March 5th—My Dear Sister since I began this letter we have moved camps twice and I have been compelled to begin again. We are now some 50 miles from where we were when I began this. We are now guarding the right wing of Our Army where we have been before this on the left. Why the chance I do not know unless it is that at Peryville our Regt. was on the left and that was where the hardest fighting took place. At Mufresboro we were on the left and there the hardest fighting and most complete victory was. Now that we are looking for Rosencranz to advance on Tullohoma, they put us on the right wing to guard the right wing of our army but I can not tell you when the fight will come off, if we have another fight here at all. The Yanks are now engaged in Digging and fortifying Murfresboro and Franklin & other points. Whether they will advance on us yet remains to be seen, though I am under the impression that they will.

One thing is very certain to my mind—they have either now got to advance on us and drive us before them or else they must soon end this war. They cannot afford to keep the men in the Field that they have and remain idle. They must whip us to end this war as they want it ended or else they must end it as we want to end it. They have passed a general Conscript act in the North and they say that it will give them 800,000 more men to crush out the rebellion. I do not believe that they will dare to attempt to enforce the conscript act. The North Western states say that they will not stand it nor will they furnish another man to carry on the war. Two months will tell how things are going to be or at least this Spring's Campaign will tell whether the war will end this year or whether it will continue as long as Abe Lincoln keeps the Presidential chair.

March 5th—Now My Dear Sister Scott I suppose that I have written to you enough of the movements of our army now of our boys. Our Regt is on outpost duty. That is, they are on picket and are not in camp where they have a chance to write & I come from them this morning in order that I might write to you for them all. Brother Tom is very well and is very well supplied with what is needed for his comfort. Cousin Cap is as jolly as any one you ever saw—fat as a little berkshire pig and ready for anything that may turn up. Frank McGuire is in fine health and as good a soldier as ever answered at roll call. Cousin Jim McGuire is also in good health. George McGehee is also in fine health and good spirits. All are ready to do duty and willing as they are now, all on Picket duty. Cousin Bob Hill quit our Company to join a Spy Comp. that was made up of one man from every Comp of the Brigade and commanded by F. G. Gordon of Comp. "A" who was promoted to Capt for Gallant conduct. On last Sunday, which was the first, Cousin Bob and one other man was detailed to get bread for the company. While they were out the Yanks came on to them and captured them so that Cousin Bob Hill is also a prisoner. He was in fine health. I received a letter from Gus[66] to Bob which I broke open and read. It was dated the 26th Jan—I regret to learn that Uncle Wileys[67] health is so bad.

I just now saw one of our Regt who talked to the man at whose house Cousin Bob was captured. He was not hurt; was eating his dinner when the Yanks came onto him. I wish you would let Uncle Wiley know as soon as possible. I tried to keep Bob from joining the Company but he thought it was a good chance to distinguish himself and joined. I hope that Bob will meet Brother John. I have not heard from John since I last wrote. I am very

---

66. Gus was Gus Hill, a son of Wiley Hill, and a brother of Bob Hill.
67. Uncle Wiley was Wiley Hill, who came to Texas with Middleton Hill. He lived in Hill's Prairie.

much afraid that our prisoners are suffering very much. It has been so very cold and the Yanks take every thing in the way of blankets from our men as well as their money and for that reason I very much fear that our men who are in the hands of the enemy are suffering.

Now Sister, you must write to me and tell me all the news from home, everything that is done there and something about every one. You have not said one word of Miss Mid[68] in any of your last letters. What is the matter? Have you and her had any falling out? If so I am very sorry. I hope you and her are still as friendly as ever.

Did you go to the concert at Houston given to the Rangers? I see it advertised in the papers. I hope you did and enjoyed yourself very much.

Give my love to all enquiring friends and especially to Uncle Tom & Aunt Scotty; also to Cousin Nish & Polly and to Miss Ruth[69] should you see her again. I have written to her twice. Tell Sister Sallie to write to me and give her my love. Brother Tom last wrote to her a few days ago. He received her letter some time since that she last wrote and was very proud indeed. Scott you must tell Cousin Alice[70] to write to me. I never was as glad to get a letter in my life as I was when I received hers. Tell Aunt Scott that I have been away from home nearly two years and would like to get a letter from her. Sister Nat has never written to me either. She has written to Brother John but not to me or Tom either. I am not complaining nor must they complain at me for I write whenever I get a chance. I am now writing while it is snowing and very disagreeable indeed. My hands are so very cold that I can scarcely hold on to my pen and form my letters. Sister, when you see any of Mrs. Shipp's family give them my regards and say to them that Maj is in fine health and that he has not heard from

68. Miss Mid was Middie Hart, who has been mentioned before.
69. Miss Ruth was Miss Ruth Ebelin who lived in Bastrop, not far from the Hills.
70. Cousin Alice was Alice Nicholson, who lived in Bastrop County.

Bob Shipp yet. Maj lets me read all the letters that he gets from his Mother and she writes a splendid letter.

Give my love to all enquiring friends and give Miss Mid when you see her a kiss for me and ask if she can return it. Tell all the negroes howdy.

Your Brother,
Bob

ROBERT EDWARD HILL TO MARY SCOTT HILL

Hd Qtrs Tex Rangers Camp
March the 25, 1863

My Dear Sister

I have just gotten permission to come into camp this morning and embrace the opportunity to write you a few lines. Our Command is out on the front doing Picket & Scouting duty and none are allowed to leave except the sick. Our boys are all well. Cap, Brother Tom, Frank & Jim McGuire, all well. Cousin George McGehee is not very well, nor very sick. Complaining with very slight fever, still he is out on the front with the command. I have heard from Brother John. Griffin made his escape from the Yanks in Illinois. They were taking them on north to Camp Douglas where they will remain untill they are exchanged. I do not know the reason why they are not immediately exchanged as I know that we have more than they have. Brother John was suffering from diarrhea. P. J. Watkins was quite sick. Some places they were treated very well and others as bad as they well could be. All quiet here. The two armies laying still looking each other in the face like two mad dogs before they begin to fight. When they will go at it again is more than I can tell. Our Regt. is ordered out tomorrow to try and get into their rear and I think we will succeed.

We have had some beautiful spring-like weather for a week but this morning a real Texas Norther is coming up suddenly and it's beginning to snow in good fashion. I rode 8 miles and got quite cold but now this evening it is very pleasant compared to this morning. Sun shining out bright. I hope it will continue and that we will not have any more cold weather as our boys have to stay out all the time without tents or anything except their blankets.

Col. Ferrill lost the letters that was sent by him at Houston. His saddle bags having been taken through mistake. Some of the letters are beginning to come to hand but none for any of us yet. I do wish you would write oftener than you do. This makes the third letter this month for me & I am sure that you, Uncle Tom, Cousin Nish, Sister Matt & others might write oftener if only to say all well and what you were doing. No news from Cousin Bob. How does Uncle Wiley take Cousin Bob being a prisoner? I fear that it will go right hard with Uncle.

It is impossible to tell now how many things are going to be if the people of the North stand the Conscript Act and make <u>Old Abe a Dictator</u>. I fear that we will be in the field another two years though I am informed that the K.G.C.s, a secret order, are determined to resist the draft. If they do, it will cause a muss. I hope they will. Griffin says that he made himself known to about 600 who had met, as an escaped prisoner and that they gave him every assistance and aided him through. I do hope before the next 6 months to see outbreaks and riots over all the North.

Pray for us and also for an Early Peace and may the lord bless and keep you all safe from harm and continue his blessing and protection to us is my daily Prayer. Give my love to all enquiring friends and tell all the negroes howdy. I have no time to write any more.

Good by,
Bob

ROBERT EDWARD HILL[71] TO MARY SCOTT HILL

Hd. Quarters Texas Rangers
Camp in Front, June 21, 1863

My Dear Sister

Once again are we placed in the front to guard the approach of the Enemy or to hide our movements from the keen eyes of our watchful enemy. We have been in the rear and on the flank for three months and our boys for the last 6 weeks have not had much to do. We have been letting our horses rest, and trying to recruit them up but forage is so very scarce that we have not improved them much.

Our Regt. is stronger now and turns out more men for duty than any time since we arrived at Bowling Green, Ky. nearly two years ago. We have no sickness now scarcely, and almost every man has a horse. There are some that you could scarcely drive away from the wagon camp with a stick but they are called Wagon dogs and have to do the duties of camp killing and cleaning of beefs and guarding the commissary stores. We have only had one man wounded in our Regt for some time. One of Company "K" was wounded last week in the head by the yanks. He is with his company now doing duty so you know that he could not have been hurt very badly.

The last letters received from home were from Cousin Nish. He had been at Houston and wrote from LaGrange on his way back home. We have written several letters but since the Enemy have so closely invested Vicksburg and Port Hudson I reckon you have not received them. Oh! How anxious we watch the movements at those places and how our hearts swell with gratitude for the successful defence thus far of those places and how we pray that He who rules the Destiny of Nations may give us a complete Decissive victory over our God-Defying enemies and ere this reaches

71. Part of this letter is lost. The context indicates that it was written Robert E. Hill

you there will be stirring times in the confederacy. Genrl. R. E. Lee is advancing upon Pensylvania & Maryland and the scene of carnage will again be in Maryland or Pennsylvania. Old Abe is calling frantically for 100,000 more men to defend the state from invasion and becomes perfectly furious because he does not get them. May the Lord of Hosts grant Genrl. Lee success. Then will we carry this war which has been waged with such hatred home to those miserable deluded wretches and make them feel the hardships of modern warfare. Times look brighter now than they have ever looked since the beginning of this unholy war, and should we loose Vicksburg and Port Hudson and Genrl. Lee should Enter Pennsylvania and infest Washington City, it would hurt them worse than it would us. But I do not believe that we will loose either Vicksburg or Port Hudson and that we will invade Washington City. General Bragg is also playing his part here. The Yanks do not want to give up Tennessee and would almost as soon give up Washington City as Nashvill. I believe that Genrl. Bragg has ordered us here to the front to cover his movements and that while he is presenting a bold front to the enemy he will throw enough of his forces to General Lee or Johnston to make them strong enough for them to effect any object they may wish to accomplish. And should General Rosecrans wish to advance here we could fight him and hold him in check for any length of time by falling back upon Shelbyvill and Tullahoma, Bridgeport and Chattanooga. Rosencrans is evidently bothered about what to do. If he reinforces Grant, he leaves all of this country open and then Genrl. Lee seems to be moving ahead as if in perfect contempt of fighting Joe Hooker and the finest army on the Planet. A few decisive victories in Maryland and they will begin to beg us to let them alone. I expect for Old Abe to call on Gov. Seymoure of New York for the Militia and I expect for Seymoure to refuse him which will bring about an open rupture between New York and the Lincoln Dynasty. The Gov. of Penn. is mad and is sailing out upon the people because they will not rush into what they well know would be perfect slaughter. I think that they are showing their good sense by staying at home I have heard that the people of that state has said that if the rebels even entered it again and they were forced to take up arms that they would enter the Southern Army but we do not want them. If they were to do that they could lay some claim to our sympathy and mercy. I would like for them just to stay at their homes and give our soldiers something to eat, keep out of the Army and attend our sick and wounded. We will walk over the track with God's blessing with perfect ease. Pray for us my Dear Sister. Pray God that we may be successful in our course for southern Liberty. Pray that your own & our loved states may never be polluted with the tread of the Yankee invaders. Pray our General may meet with success at Vicksburg, Port Hudson in Maryland and Penn. and finally that we who are [*Letter ends abruptly*]

JAMES H. HILL[72] TO MARY SCOTT HILL

Camp Bradison Near Donelsonvill, July 1,1863

Miss M. S. Hill

Dear Sister

I have not heard from home since I left Brenham and have been going ever since about the fourth of March and I have written to you, sister Matt, to Mother to Cousin Nish and from none of you have I received a scratch of a pen. But I still live in hope of hearing from you all soon. The reason why I have not got my letters is because I have not stayed at one place long enough for to get a letter so I will try and give you a consolidated report of travailing and our fighting and our travel so you can see what we have done. Well

72. James H. Hill was a brother of Mary Scott Hill. He was not a member of Terry's Texas Rangers.

when I last wrote to you it was at Simsfort on the Atchafalaya. We started from there on the 14th of June, came down the River (Atchafalaya) and went to what is called Morgans ferry. Crossed the River (Atchafalaya) and went to what is called False River. It was the Missisippi River once upon a time. We tried to kick up a fight but did not succeed in doing so we then started and came to Plaquemine on the Miss River. There we burnt three Steamboats and captured about sixty prisoners. The gunboats came up and shelled us off. We lost one man out of Capt James Martins Cavalry by the name of Rane Oyton. We then started down to Thibeauxdevill (where we was last year) and captured one hundred and fifty prisoners and a yankie store that had a little of every thing in it. I got me a pair of boots out of it. We then went to Bayou Bluff where we captured foure hundred and fifty prisoners and about one thousand stand of arms, also one thirty-two pound cannon, two twenty-four pounders and one twelve pound [Howitzer] and provisions accordingly; also two Lococmotives. While we (I mean our Regiment) were doing this, General Moody with his command and General Tom Green with his Brigade and the Second Regiment of the Arizona Brigade (Col Baylors Regt) attacked them at the Bay. They captured about twelve hundred prisoners, also five Siege Cannon and about one million dollars worth of Property (belonging to the U. S.) We then turned round, came back to Thibeauxdevill then started up Bayou LaForche to Dondsonville where there was about five Hundred Federal in a Fort.

And last Sunday morning (which was the 28th) just about three o'clock in the morning we attacked them but was driven back with a heavy loss out of our Regiment. We lost Col. Joseph Phillips Killed, we reckon. Col. G. T. Madison, slightly wounded & Maj. Ridley killed. Lt. W. K. Walker was shot dead; the ball struck him in the forehead. Our Regt went in with one hundred and fifty and it lost fifty besides the wounded which we got out which is not many I assure you. Sister I reckon it was a good thing that I was not in the fight for I reckon I would have been killed too.

Now you will want to know why I was not in the fight. This is the reason. I was detailed to stay at Bayou Bluff with Capt Turner to help with the Comissary stores that was captured there. As I have wrote you a pretty long letter and, on yankie paper at that, and have two or three quires of it at that, I will close by saying that you must answer it as soon as you get this and let me know how all is at home and all of the news. Do not let any body read this except Sister Matt or Mother.

Sister I feel like I ought to write more to you but I do not see how I can do it for my mind is on our Col. Maj. and especially Billy Walker whom you heard me speak of while I was at home. Our Col. left his home in Maryland to come and fight our Battle and now is no more. Sister if you have any way I want you to send me more two or three white shirts and some drawers. The white shirts I want them as nice as possible for in going with the Col. I want to look like somebody. The way I am dressed now I know you would laugh. I will describe myself. Well in the first place I have a nice pair of boots, a cloth coat with posson on it (captured from Federal Officer,) the pants I left Home in and a great long pair of stockings. Checked shirt—I have one with waggons but have not seen them since the 14th of last month.

Tell Miss Jennie[73] that I would like to see her mighty well. Also tell her some rascal stole that lock of hair that she gave me. He stoled twenty dollars also. Excuse all mistakes for I know there is a great many and write to your Brother.

J. H. Hill

73. Miss Jennie was Miss Jennie Edmondson, who was a friend of the Hills.

JOHN W. HILL TO MARY SCOTT HILL

Camp Silver Creek
Near Rome, Floyd Co. Ga, Aug. 15, 1863

Miss M. S. Hill, Bastrop

Dear Sister

Another opportunity presents for me to write to you as Charles Caldwell[74] is going to start home in the morning. This leaves us all well except Cap. He has been sick for several dayes but is up again. He is staying at a house out of camp where there is a nice young lady. We heard yesterday from Bob Hill. He is over in Middle Tennessee. He was at Lebanon. When last heard from he was in good health. Sam Watkins is at Courtland Ala sick. He was quite sick when last heard from. There is several others of our Company sick but none of them dangerous. Ed & P. R. Kennedy,[75] Robert Shipp, John B. Rector,[76] Wm Davis,[77] Sam Pipes,[78] Rome Campbell. All the rest of the Company is in fine health. There is a rumor in camp that we will leave here soon and I hope that we will for I had rather be in active service. We have five Roll Calls per day. Inspection of arms & horses at 9 p.m. Drill from four to five. Dress Parade at Sun-down. I have not been out of camp but three times sinse we have been here which will be four weeks tomorrow. This is a soldiers rest. We have plenty of fruit of all kinds. Some the finest peaches that I ever saw. There is plenty apples, pears, quince and other fruit in aboundance. Plenty vegatables but they sell them very high. Irish potatoes are worth six to eight dollars per bushel. The wheat & corne are fine. The corne is getting too hard to ear except that which was planted late. We have had plenty of

74. Charlie Caldwell was from Bastrop County. He had at this time gotten a discharge.
75. Ed and P. R. Kennedy were from Bastrop County, Texas.
76. John B. Rector was from Bastrop County.
77. William Davis was from Travis County.
78. Sam Pipes was also from Travis County.

raine of late. It has been raining every day or two sinse we have been here. We have had several letters from our relations down in Ga. They were all well when last heard from except cousin Cole Seay. They sent us a box filled withe good things—three bottles of Old Peach & Honey. We have heard that Cousin Tom after the fall of Vicksburg bought him a mule and started home. Hope that he will make it through safe and that long before this arrives, he has given you all a happy surprise. I tryed to get a furlow to go down to Griffen but there was no use in my trying. I have not been absent from the Company more than two days sinse I have been in Service except while I was a prisoner. I have been in every fight that the Company has been in. Other men though get furlows and go and stay as long as they like. I never intend to try to get to leave of absence any more except if I am sick or wounded. We have a protracted meeting going on in Camps. It has been going on for about three weeks. There has been about thirty converted and about sixty seeking religion. Tomorrow is Sunday and they are going to administer the Sacrement to those that have joined the church. We have had Minasters from all the different denominations preaching to us. Mr. Bunting, our Chaplain, has been laboring very hard to get up a revival in the Regt. There is nothing new here that would interest you. The yanks have not attempted to cross the Tenn River and Genl. Bragg withe his army is laying waiting for the enemy either to fight or run. Either of which he'd do to perfection. We have nothing late from Va. Dr. Yates[79] is up at Ringold, surgeon of the Hospital there. Brother Bob got a letter from him. He and Cousin Lizzy were bothe well. Frank McGuire got a letter a few dayes ago from Cousin William Walker.[80] He had been home and he reported all of Ma's relatives

79. Dr. Yates married a cousin of the Hills. She is the Cousin Lizzie who is later mentioned. They lived in La Grange.

80. William Walker was the son of Mrs. Middleton Hill's brother. Aunt Maria Caldwell, John Caldwell, and John Glasscock were all relatives of Mrs. Middleton Hill's. Uncle Alexander was an uncle of Mrs. Hill's. They all lived in Alabama.

well. We have seen William Walker several times. He is 1st Lt in Cavalrey Company. Aunt Maria Cardwell is dead. She has been dead about three monthes. John Cardwell & John Glasscock was at Vicksburg when it fell. We have not heard whether they come out safe or not. Uncle Alexander Glasscock is married again. He married a young lady. I do not know her name.

Scott I want you to tell Ma to send me some money the first good chance that presents itselfe. I am out of money. When I got back from the Northe I had to pay $102.50 for a six shooter. I have never Bet a cent on cards or anything else sinse. I have been in the armey which is more than a majority can say. Boots are worth from 50 to 75 dollars, hats from 25 to 50 and every thing else in proportion. I heard a man say in town a few dayes ago that he sold ten dollars in gold for one hundred and twenty dollars in Confederate money. You must Excuse all mistakes and write soon and a long letter. My Love to all the relations and friends and axcept a good portion for yourselfe.

Your Brother,
John W. Hill

Crocket says tell all of the Darkeys Howdy for him and his love to Lizer.

JOHN W. HILL TO MARY SCOTT HILL

I had my picture taken at Greevill and will send it to you if I do not find some Magnanimous gal that will accept it and the giver to boot. We have had a good deal of cold weather here of late. Had snow on 21st, 22nd of last month that was Eight or ten inches in depth. As for rain it is an every day business. The peach trees were all in bloom at the time of the snow so the fruit was all destroyed.

We left Cousin Geo T. McGehee in Greevill sick as we came through there. He had fever but I hope that it is nothing serious. We left him at a good place where he will be well taken care of. He will come around at the Camp as soon as he gets well. Say to Scotty Phillips that I never received her letter. If I had I would have answered it. I saw Nat Rives this morning. He is well. Wm Sayers went through Va to see his relations. All the boyes from our country are well.

Jno. W. Hill

ROBERT EDWARD HILL TO MARY SCOTT HILL

Hd. Quarters, Texas Rangers
Camp Near Rome Ga, August 24, 1863

My Dear Sister

A few days ago I wrote to Uncle Tom & Aunt Scott by Charlie Caldwell and Brother John wrote to you and now that I have another opportunity of writing and sending by hand. I know that you all are very anxious about us and we let no opportunity pass without writing letters that maybe you may get some of them.

When I wrote to Uncle Tom, Cousin Cap had been quite sick but is now in camp again. He looks somewhat worsted but is gaining strength as fast as could be expected. The other boys of us are all well. Mrs. Shipps boys are both sick, nothing serious. I have the fevers stopped on Bob and Maj is out at a house close to camp. He is doing well, will be able to be in camp again in a few days. Hugh Allen has been sick ever since he arrived here. In fact he was sick before he reached us. He is up though now but looks very bad. He took a notion to turn back in Missippi and gave a portion of the mail that he had with him to some one to mail and all the letters to me were lost or done something with. I never received any. Uncle Toms & Cousin Nish's letters came safe to hand and all were read with eagerness. Hugh is very sorry that my letters were lost and so am I but I will not complain. I know that you all at home think of me and write whenever you think you can get a letter through.

I do sincerely hope that Cousin Tom Anderson reached home safe & sound and gave you all relief from the distressing uncertainty of how he fared while in Vicksburg. He looked for Cousin Tom to visit us untill I received a letter from Cousin Billy Seay[81] stating that Tom had crossed the Missippi and had gone home. I would like very much to be there with him and enjoy home for a while once more, but such are the fates of war that we must remain yet in the Field.

Sister we have been in this camp for over one month resting and recruiting our horses and during the whole time we have had a protracted meeting going on. The Chaplain of Our Regt. with other Ministers of different denominations have labored by day and by night and their labors have been blessed by the Lord in that a good number have professed their sins forgiven...I think about 40. A large number of back sliders have been reclaimed...50. And now there are a large number who are enquiring the way of Salvation...100...and seem to be in earnest and yet strange to say there has been no what I would call Revival Sermons Preached but a general seriousness seems to have taken hold upon the Regt. and men have gone forward from convictions of duty. There has never at any time been any excitement but the work has gradually increased, widened and deepened untill the entire Regt. is more or

81. Cousin Billy Seay married a niece of Middleton Hill's.

less under the influence of the spirit of God. You can scarcely now hear any oath when too months ago nothing else was heard. Very little card playing and although they are making Peach Brandy all round us and the boys have free access to it, you do not see any drinking nor no rowdiness any where.

I believe that our Regt. stands head and shoulders above any other in this department for gallantry on the Field, for our good behavior while in camp and for intelligence among the men—I am Proud of the Texas Rangers. I am glad that the people at home are proud of us and I hope & trust in god that the day may soon come when this war shall be over and we all meet once again around our fireside and family altar with no hated yankee to molest nor disturb us.

In my letter to Uncle Tom I expressed my fears that Cousin Bobbie had been captured again by the enemy. He left us in Tennessee and went on a scout into Ky and was sent by the Officer in command of the party to reconnoitre the forces around Franklin Ky and Gellatin Tenn. Up to the time that I wrote to Uncle I had not heard from him. I have since learned that Cousin Bob is safe and is with a party of our Regt and a portion of the 11th Texas who are up in Tennessee watching the movements of the Enemy and bushwhacking them every chance they can get.

And now my Dear Sister, the hour of Trial is coming for the South. The time that is to try the Patriotism of every man—The Enemy are gathering their Hosts for a final crushing act, and we must meet them. You must not become discouraged at nothing which may happen. All shall work out right in the end. Charleston may be taken, Richmond may be evacuated, Mobile may fall into the hands of the enemy and still we are not conquored. I believe that the Lord of Hosts is pouring out his spirit upon our armies for his own Good Purpose and I believe that when the mighty shock of armies meet again the shout of deliverance will go up from the hearts of the people in these Southern States. "Let not your hearts be troubled. Ye Believe in God." Believe also in his special Providence and that all things shall work together for good to those who love and serve him in spirit & in Truth. Here holding the Middle Ground may we have your prayers for our success and for our safety, and for a speedy return of peace to our distracted and desolated land. Then can we return to our loved homes— and receive the love and congratulations of our Friends at home and rest in peace.

Our Boys are in fine health. Brother Tom, Brother John, Cousin Cap, George Mcgehee, Jim & Bud Mcguire are all in fine health and are not on the front. Consequently they cannot write home and this must suffice for us all. They all send their love to you and to all enquiring friends.

I received a letter from Cousin Betty Seay who lives in Griffin Ga. She says that she had just received a letter from Cousin Tom. He was in fine health and anxious for the yanks to keep on making their attacks. She says that Cousin Tom was in fine Spirits and seemed perfectly confident that they could whip any number of the Yanks that they could bring against them. The People of Ga are helping us in every way that they can. Cousin Betty[82] says that every evening in Griffin prayers are offered up for our safety and especially for Genrl Whartons command.

There is a great Revival of Religion going on in the infantry. Hundreds, yes, thousands have professed Religion and the work is still going on. Our Chaplain says that they cannot supply the Army with Bibles and hymn books and Religious tracts such is the great demand for them. Do you think such men who are thus favored of God can be conquored? I tell you history will soon hear the thundering of Genl Lees Cannon answering "No." This revival has not yet extended to any of the Cavalry that I have heard of. But still I do not think that there is as much wickedness in our Regt as there used to be. At night it resembles more a camp meeting than it used to. Seated around the fires you can see groups of men singing, sometimes sacred songs but most usually such songs as *Anna Laura Lorena, Bold Soldier Boy* and *Home Sweet*

82. Cousin Betty was Mrs. Billey Seay, who was a niece of Middleton Hill's.

Home. The beginning of the end is drawing nigh. How strange it would seem if this army should become a great christian army and the battles that are now going on around Vicksburg should be the Great battle of Armeggeddon that shall lift this young nation at once to the proud standard of Gods chosen people and we enter upon our Glorious course. You will recollect that last December I then said I believed that the battles that would decide the present contest would be fought between Vicksburg & Jackson. Well the Yanks did not go as I thought they would but evidently they have concentrated their whole force there and although they have succeeded for a time now they have been checkmated and the game is about to wind up. I do not believe that Genl Grant can extricate himself from his position without heavy loss.

And now Sister the first time you see Mrs. Camp[83] tell her that her Brother in Va is in very bad health. I was told that the physicians thought that he would never be able to walk again. Tell her that her half brother has not joined the Yankee Army and that her father wrote to Genl. Morgan for permission to come home. Genl. Morgan granted the permission and his son went after him with two horses and the Yanks kept the old man, his son and his two horses. Such is the generosity of the Yanks and the old man is still with them but is anxious to get away from them.

And now Sister I believe that I have told you all the news that I could think of and some was conjecture of my own with reference to the movements of our forces. You must tell Cousin Nish that Capt. Ben Tolliver is Dead. He died with pneumonia near Wartrace about 6 weeks ago. His brother paid $5,000 for a substitute and has gone home. Tell Cousin Alice that I answered her letter as soon as I received hers and I hope she will get it. Tell her she must learn to play a piece for me if I live to get back home. Give my love to all enquiring friends, to Uncle Tom and to Aunt Scott, to Cousin Nish and to Cousin Polly. Let Uncle Wiley know that he is not forgotten by us in camp, that Cousin Bob is well. Started

83. Mrs. Camp lived in Bastrop County.

day before yesterday into Ky with the scouts. Tell the negroes all howdy and tell them that we often think of them in camps. Mrs. J. G. John & George Eblen and all the enquiring friends who may ask after us, present to them our kindest and most affectionate regards. And now to our best of Mothers and all the family who are at home, we send much love to you all and ask an entrust in your supplication for our welfare and safe return home.

Your Brother,
Bob

P. S. Tell Uncle Tom that Cousin Betty Seay says in her letter that she had heard that Cousin Miles McGehee[84] had taken the Oath of Allegiance to the Lincoln Government to save his property. Cousin Betty is very severe in her denunciations of him and says that she loved him like a brother but she was very bitter upon such as would take the Oath to save a few darkies, and then perhaps lose them. She says that Uncle Billy[85] and Aunt Emily were well a few days ago and that Aunt Ann[86] was still in Aberden and was well; that Cousin Georgia and Cousin Sue Blanton[87] were gone to Aunt Emily's; that Henry E. Williamson and Cousin Sue were well and all the relations in Ga. I met with a young man in the 2nd Cavalry the other day who was acquainted with all of the kinfolk down about Cousin Meriwether Hill and Cousin Wiley Hill in Ga. He said they were all well and in good spirits and that crops were never more promising. The Good Lord has smiled upon us in a bountiful harvest everywhere I can hear from. The crops of wheat and rye very fine indeed here. Corn here is very backward...some of it not half-leg high and very little is waist high though they

---

84. Cousin Miles McGehee was a cousin of Middleton Hill. He lived in Georgia.
85. Uncle Billy and Aunt Emily- Aunt Emily was Amelia Walton Hill, a sister of Middleton Hill. Uncle Billey was Wm. Gresham, her husband. They lived in Lexington, Georgia.
86. Aunt Ann was Nancy Ann Scott Hill, who was a sister of Middleton Hill.
87. Cousin Georgia and Sue Blanton were nieces of Middleton Hill. They lived in Barnesville, Georgia.

have had fine rains and beautiful growing weather. The reason that they are so late here is the people did not know what to do on the falling back of Genl Bragg from Murfresboro. They had no idea that we would hold this country and they did not prepare their lands untill confidence was established that we would give them another fight before giving up the finest grain country in Tennessee. The farmers are beginning to cut their wheat and rye now and the fields look very pretty but very few oats raised on account of scarcity of seed but what I have seen look very fine. Grass & clover lots very fine indeed and, in fact, I think the Yanks will have to give up the idea of starving us out. What plan they will fall on next to deceive the North remains for some Yankee genius in inventing his to develop. My paper is about give out & I will close.

Your Brother,
Bob

ROBERT EDWARD HILL TO MARY SCOTT HILL[88]

Hd. Quarters, Texas Rangers
Camp near French Broad River, Jan 8, 1864

My Dear Sister

The last letter I wrote you was in Nov. I also wrote you by Judge Terry from Cherokee Springs near Ringgold Ga. I hope you have received them.

I was in hopes at that time that we would get transferred to the West side of the Missippi but I fear now that we will not get

88. This letter is unsigned but the context shows that it was written by Dr. R. E. Hill.

on that side of the river until the war is ended which I do not see much prospects for at this time.

General Wharton went to Richmond Va to get us over but I suppose failed and we are now in East Tennessee attached to General Longstreet.

Our boys had a very hard time on their trip in Middle Tennessee, had hard riding and hard fighting to do. Our boys all got out safe except Bill Simms and Maj Shipp. I do not think that they are captured but I think they are remaining over there bushwhacking and capturing and paroling small parties of Yankees. We have about 25 or 30 men in Middle Tennessee that got cut off in scouts and in small parties. You can say to Mrs. Shipp that I do not think Maj is captured.

Our boys are all well with the exception of Brother John. He was ordered to hospital in Georgia while we had Knoxville besieged. I think Brother John is with some of the relatives in Georgia. He spoke of going to Griffin and I expect he is there. Brother Tom is here. His health has not been very good for some two weeks but he is still with the company and does duty. He is now going on picket. Cousin Cap is as fat as a bear and in fine health. Cousin Jim McGuire[89] started this morning on a forty days furlough. General Longstreet has issued an order to furlough 5 men out of every 100, and Jim McGuire, I. V. Jones[90] and David S. Combs[91] drew the Furlough for Co. "D." Cousin Jim[92] had gone to Mobile & Tuscaloosa. Brother John, when he came back out of Tennessee, went down to Tuscaloosa to see the relations. They were very glad indeed to see him and gave him everything he wanted at that time. He saw Aunt Mary Moody[93] and stayed several days at Uncle Pearce Walkers[94] They are very anxious for us to come and

89. Cousin Jim McGuire was a nephew of Mrs. Middleton Hill's.
90. I.V. Jones was from Travis County.
91. David S. Combs was from Hayes County.
92. Cousin Jim was Jim McGuire.
93. Aunt Mary Moody was a sister of Mrs. Middleton Hill's.
94. Uncle Pearce Walker was the brother of Mrs. Middleton Hill.

see them when ever we can come. He also saw John Strong and Mrs. Strong[95] says that she would rather see mother than any person on earth. Cousin Frank is well is now with the company. Frank is a good boy and always ready for duty. Cousin George McGehee is rather under the weather from Rheumatism in his knees. He is out in the country.

The boys are generally all well. Billy Nicholson[96] was wounded a few days ago...slight wound in the top of the head. Dick Purgin was wounded the same day...shot through the face. N. J. Allen was killed. The wounded boys are doing very well. They are at a good place and are receiving every attention that can be given to men. We have had a good deal of hard fighting to do since we came into East Tennessee. The day before Christmas we had to fight nearly all day and the day after Christmas was the same. We did not fight any Christmas day but was saddled up all day expecting the Enemy would attack us but they were good enough to let us alone that day.

95. Mr. and Mrs. Strong were some old friends of Mrs. Middleton Hill's who lived in Alabama.
96. Billy Nicholson was from Bastrop County.

ROBERT EDWARD HILL[97] TO MARY SCOTT HILL

Hd. Quarters, Texas Rangers
January 10, 1864

Dear Scott

We have had the coldest spell of weather I ever saw. Snow on the ground now and while I write it is freezing cold but I am sitting out in the open air with a big log fire in my shirt sleeves. I have no over coat and I have not been able to get one for love nor money. I did not go on the trip into Middle Tennessee; consequently I am not as well provided for the cold as some of the other boys. I have one blanket. The Yanks took all my blankets at Mursfresboro. When Brother John went down into Georgia he left me two of his blankets. I have one pair of good cotton socks the rest are more holey than righteous. I have not had a pair of boots this winter though I think I will get a pair in a few days.

If anything whips us it will be from desertion. Our troops are so badly clothed, in fact almost naked. They are deserting and going home. The Tennessee troops are deserting more than any other. I believe that our Regt. is better clothed and better prepared for winter than any other Regt in this army. Our Qtr Master has gone to Richmond Va now after a supply of clothing. The Railroad will soon be running to Morristown and we will soon be able to get everything we need from Virginia.

I think we will get through the winter now without much more fighting as everything is froze up. The ground is now frozen so hard that a heavy loaded wagon makes no impression. Our troops at Morristown have made their winter quarters and are making themselves very comfortable.

I am told that nearly one half of the Texas Brigade are barefooted yet the Texas troops are the most cheerful and the most

97. This letter is unsigned, but the context indicates that it was written by Dr. Hill.

hopeful of any troops in the field. If General Bragg is sent to the West side of the River, Gen. Wharton I think will certainly go with him. If he does we will yet get a crop. I should like very much to get once more where I could hear from home occasionally and once more could get to visit the old Loved Place of home.

Next September will be 3 years since we were mustered into the service & I think that they will certainly grant those who may chance to live out the time a leave of absence long enough to go home. The time seems long but will soon run off and perhaps you may see some of us then next Fall if not sooner. If Col Harrison keeps up the mail by sending two married men home to carry letters and bring letters back I think Brother Tom will be one of the next. The old Col came very near deciding on him this time and there were others here who had claims and he decided on one from Gonzales and one from near—Waco Mr. Houston and Mr. Sanders.

And now my dear Scott I hardly know how to bring this to a close. So many things I could tell you if I was there and so little news to write about the army, and the movements of our armies as everything seems to be laying quiet, gathering their strength for another conflict in the opening of spring. I look for hard fighting when the spring opens unless it be because of the Yankees time being out in the spring. All of the 3 years their time is out in March & April; I do not believe that they went to fight much more.

I heard the other day that the Yankee Congress had taken a vote on a bill to send commissioners to Richmond. Ten were for peace on any terms, 64 were for peace if the South would consent to come back into the union and consent to live under the Rule of the North and 84 were for whipping us into submission. So it seems that they are resolved at last upon subjugation. Better will it be for us to meet death than to submit to them for you know not what the devils will do when once they are turned loose.

And now my Dear Sister I ask you and all loved ones at home to continue your prayers to Our Heavenly Father for his preserving kindness over us while Death has held its carnival around us. That he may guard, guide and protect us through this war. You must give my love to our Dear Mother, Sister and all the Family. Give my love to Uncle & Aunt, Cousin Nish & Cousin Pal, and to all enquiring friends at home. Give my love and a kiss to Miss Mid. You never said a word about her in your letters

Tell Uncle Wiley that Cousin Bob is again a Prisoner and was at Camp Douglas. The last we heard from him he was well and in good spirits. I fear it will be a good while before we see Cousin Bob as they are not exchanging Prisoners at this time. You can say to Mrs. Shipp that the reason she does not get letters from her boys is because Maj is over in Middle Tennessee and that Bob was suffering from bronchitis so much that I gave him a certificate to keep him off duty and he is now absent from the command staying at private house.

I have been trying to get Bob a position down in Ga in the Qtr. Master Dept.

John W. Hill to Mary Scott Hill

Anderson C. H. S. C
Apr 8, 1864

Miss M. S. Hill
Bastrop

Dear Sister

As we are going to remain here to day as it is fast day, I thought that I would write to you. I received your letter of Nov. 1st whilest I was at Rome Ga. I wrote several letters home whilest I was there. We left Rome on the 10th of March. Came through Leworth, Canton, Alfereta, Loreneburg and got to Athens on the 17th. I went to see Blanton Hill's Family.[98] Stayed all night withe them. They were very glad to see me and treated me with the greatest kindness; they asked a thousand questions about you all. She has two Sons in Service: Frank & Blanton Hill. One is a Major; the other is a Capt in the regular Service.

There oldest daughter married a Mr. Nobles. She is also at their plantation. Susan, their youngest daughter, is at home. She is very pretty & a very nice young lady. They asked me to give you all their love the first time that I wrote to you all. The next day I went down to see Uncle Billy & Aunt Emley.[99] I got there after dark and walked into the dining room without letting any one know that I was there. When I walked in, Aunt was setting in the corner & Uncle was standing in the middle of the room. He had been at work at the mill, was covered withe flour and had on what we would style in Texas a two-storey hat which looked like it had a lick on top which had lowered it to half mast and inclined the top to the front. When I let them know who I was, one got hold of my right and the other my left hand and a heartier welcome I

98. Blanton Meade Hill married his cousin Elizabeth Ann Hill, who was also a first cousin of Middleton Hill's. They lived in Athens, Georgia.

99. Aunt Emily was Amelia Hill, a sister of Middleton Hill. She married William Gresham, who is referred to as Uncle Billy.

never received before in my life. Found them all well. I could not get but a two dayes pass so I had to leave them the next day at two in the evening. I could not have enjoyed myself better if I had been at home. Aunt Emley is one of the best women I ever saw. She would have loaded my horse down withe clothes and eatables if I would have let her.

We left Athens on the 20th. Passed through Donelsvill & Hartwell Ga, Anderson & Greenville SC and when we got in one mile of the N. C. line on the mountains, we met a courier saying that the Brigade would be on in a few dayes. We came back to the foot of the mountains and collected forage and waited untill they came up . All the boyes are well but many that were with the Regt when I left were not to be seen. Some of them have fallen nobly fighting for their Country & all that they held dear. Some had been taken by cursed yankeys and are probably at this moment suffering from the inhumane treatment of our Enemy in some loathsome prison.

R. R. Shipp has been ordered to report to the Q. M. at Greenvill Tenn. He will be asigned to post duty on account of his healthe. He is not with the Company. B. C. Giles[100] will also be assigned to post duty on account of his eyes. He is not withe the Company.

Brother & Cousin Cap got a pass whilest we were at Greeville SC and have gone down into Ga to see the relations. They met us at Athens. The people here are very kind. I have been treated better since I have been in SC than any where since we gave up Middle Tenn. That is, with people of course, there is good and bad in every state.

There is several of the boys that have got letters from home written in January. You must excuse all mistakes. My love to all the relations and friends and axcept the same for yourselfe

Your Brother,
Jno W. Hill

100. B. C. Giles was from Travis County.

Robert Edward Hill to Mary Scott Hill

Camp Near Resaca Ga
April 29, 1864

My Dear Sister

The last letter that I expect you received from me was dated some time in January while we were encamped near Morristown in east Tennessee. I have written to you since but do not have much hope that they have reached you. The couriers by whom you write never come to our Regt. Now and then we get a letter that has been brought over and put into some Post Office on this side of the Father of Waters and, after having wandered over many miles and been remailed some half dozen times, we accidently catch up with it. More especially was this the case while we were in East Tennessee for then we were cut off from all the rest of the Confederacy. I could not even get letters from friends and relations here in Ga. Still we must not let these things discourage us and prevent us from writing but write as often as possible. For fear that you have received no letter from me and at the risk of being tedious I will take up our doings and wanderings from January. At the time I wrote you it was very cold and continued so throughout the whole time we remained in East Tennessee. We had a great deal of hard fighting to do in order to sustain ourselves and our horses. The entire population of East Tennessee (with a few exceptions) are strong for the Union. They are poor, ignorant and unprincipled; the men degraded, corrupt and the women prostitutes and of easy virtue. Of course there are some honorable exceptions but I have never seen a country so generally corrupt and degraded, and they have met the reward which their crimes deserve: Respected by neither party they have been robbed of every thing—of their corn, meat, hay, fodder, their chickens, turkeys, ducks, geese, beegums. Everything good for man or horse has been taken. Now you may be ready to say we treated them too bad but when I tell you that these same people, while we had the Yankess surrounded on every side but the South side, worked like ants pressing everything that the Secesh had and opening everything that they thought they could open to take to the Yanks at night to keep them from starving into a surrender until reinforcements could be sent to them. If you thought we treated them too bad before hearing this, I think you will change your mind now and say we treated them about right. I tell you My Dear Sister it would have made the hair stand on your head to have heard some of those women curse the Rebels and wish them in the hottest place of the infernal regions. The people in East Tennessee are bound to suffer. There is no help for it, for I do not believe that we left corn enough in the country to more than plant the crops much less to make bread. They have some wheat but there must of necessity be much suffering among the women & children. No meat, no bread. I do not know how they will sustain until this cruel struggle is over. Had it not been necessary to remain in East Tennessee as long as we did, humanity would have demanded that the country should have been left two months before we did, as it is the enemy that can not subsist his troops there and we can concentrate on other points that are weak having no fear of a foray in East Tennessee. We left there about the last of March and came across the Mountains into North Carolina through Buncombe County and such another trip I hope I may never be called upon to make. We had to convey three days rations for our horses on horseback or else do without it and it snowed on us all the way over the mountains (the snow was fifteen inches deep on a stump) and I believe that it is snowing there to day. Mountains, mountains, nothing but mountains on every side. For three days not a living soul hardly to be seen except those riding right ahead of you or just behind you; the snow falling thick and fast and no house in which any one lived except one place (the warm Springs) and hardly room enough to build one. The third day we arrived at Ashvill N. C., a very nice town where once again the fluttering of white cambric told us we were in a civilized community. Laughing lovely faces once more greeted us as victors of the East Tennessee Campaign. Our transit then was one continued ovation through North Carolina and down into South Carolina through Greenvill and Anderson Districts. We met with hearty reception every where. We camped and rested two days at each of the last named places. Cousin George T. McGehee having been quite sick, I left him in Greenvill South Carolina in the hands of some ladies, one a refugee from Louisiana and the other from Charleston. They promised me that they would take good care of Cousin George untill he would be able to travel on the cars. I have heard from him since I left him and he was improving, able to walk about. I will expect him up on the cars in a few days. After we left Anderson we then turned across into Georgia and came through Athens where we [were] welcomed by every one and all seemed to vie with each other in extending to us their hospitality. We have some relatives at Athens and Brother John and myself enjoyed our stay of almost two days very much indeed. Brother Tom and Cousin Cap left us at Greenvill with permission to go in advance and they went down to see Aunt Emily and Uncle Billy Grisham. After leaving Athens we were ordered to Marietta Georgia we made the trip in four days, nothing occurring on the march worth mentioning. We expected to remain at Mareitta for a while and recruit but were ordered to this place where we now are recruiting our horses and resting the men, preparing ourselves for the shock of arms that must soon come on in our front. Brother Tom & Cousin Cap caught up with the command at Marietta. They report that they had a very pleasant time indeed at Uncle Billys and says the old folks were well and all of our relations in Oglethrope are in good living condition. While I was in Athens I learned from our relations there that the Yanks had been at Aberdeen Missippi and that Aunt Anne[101] had been made to feel the insults of our hated foe. They have nearly ruined Aunt Ann's place and had taken off

101. Aunt Ann was Nancy Ann Scott Hill, a sister of Middleton Hill. She married General Elisha Strong.

a good many of Uncle Elissa's fellows had treated them so bad. Nearly all had made their escape and returned home. The Yanks are putting the negroes into Regt. and putting them where they have to do very hard work putting up fortifications, giving them half rations and treating them like brutes.

Sister Scott, when I reached this place I wrote to Cousin Tom Anderson who is now at Dalton, a place fifteen miles above here, to come down and see us and he immediately came. I assure you we were very glad to see him. I had not seen Cousin Tom since we first went into Ky nearly three years ago. Cousin Tom looks very well indeed and was very glad to see us. He is now with the same command that he was when captured at Vicksburg. He could only stay with us one night and day but he asked a thousand questions that we could not write in a letter as that you had failed to give us information. Cousin Tom says the troops in the front are in the very best of spirits and are waiting patiently to welcome the Enemy when ever they feel disposed to begin the Carnival of Death. From all I can learn our army is in better trim than they have ever been and what is still better we can put more muskets in a fight than we have ever been able to do in this Dept. I do not think that the issue here will be doubtful. We feel confident that a Just God will give us the victory.

We have the news here of a glorious victory in Louisiana in which Genl E. K. Smith almost destroyed the 13th Army Corps of Banks. I only hope it may be a signal as is reported. We have also the news of a victory in N. Carolina in which we captured some twenty-five hundred prisoners, among them a good many negro troops. You have no doubt heard of the gallant deeds of the Murat of the war, Gen N. B. Forrest, and his victories in West Tennessee and in Ky. Gen. John H Morgan is again in the field with a part of his old command. He will no doubt do the Enemy a deal of harm. He will operate in Western Va and from there into Ky. His men are all determined to pay the yanks for the treatment which their gallant leader received whilst a prisoner in their hands in Ohio. Speaking of prisoners, I may as well say here that we have heard nothing from cousin Bob direct for some time. Capt. White of our Regt. was captured while on the raid in Middle Tennessee and writes from Johnson Island in Lake Erie mentioning the death of some of our Regt in Northern prisons, none of whom you know, and states that all the rest were well. We infer that Cousin Bob is well. There has been an exchange of prisoners going on at City Point near Richmond and we have been in hopes of seeing Cousin Bob exchanged but he has not reached us yet. We hope that it will not be long before all our prisoners are exchanged.

And now My Dear Sister the most painful part of my letters and I wish you to communicate the sad intelligence yourself to Mrs. Shipp. On the trip into Middle Tennessee, Maj Shipp with several others were sent on a scout under Lts. Baylor & Davis. They were cut off by the enemy and could not come out with the command. Seeing all chances to return at that was impossible, they returned and went into the Mountains above Sparta to prevent being captured. They remained there untill everything got quiet and then commenced scouting into Middle Tennes and into the southern part of Ky trying to get all the information possible and believing that it would not be long before Bragg's whole army would be in Middle Tennessee.

About the first of March our party attacked a party of yanks near Sparta killing a good many of them and whipping them badly. Lt. Davis was wounded and after the fight our boys got him to a house. The next day some 5 or 6 went back to see how he was getting along and, while there, some two hundred men belonging to Col. Stokes renegade Tennessians and all his men Tennessians surrounded the house. They were led there by one of the men who lived in the neighborhood. They demanded the surrender of the party and promised them if they would surrender that they should be treated as prisoners of war. And no sooner than they had surrendered and the infamous wretches had got possession of all their arms than they began to shoot them down. After killing the party they then went into the house where Lt. Davis was lying on a bed wounded, took him out of the bed, carried him our into the yard and shot him. Maj Shipp was one of the ill-fated party. Now my Dear Sister you can say to Mrs. Shipp and the family that they have the sympathies of our entire Regt. Maj was as gallant a boy as ever lived and had a soul as noble as ever throbbed in the breast of any one. Our Regt. will give them no quarter when and wherever we may meet them. This painful news I received from one who lives near Sparta, an old white headed citizen who had to run from his home in order to save his life. He knew all the boys and had been with them a few days before this sad tragedy was enacted. He was to have been their guide to bring them out of Tennessee.

You can also say to Mrs. Shipp that owing to Bobs health not being able to stand active service in the field I got him ordered to report to Quarter Master Dept. at Greenvill. The last I heard from him he was with some relations that are refugees from this state about Alpin at Fair Play in South Carolina. I think Bob had been ordered to Atlanta and was then on his way to that place. He has promised to write whenever he goes. His throat was still quite sore and whenever he would get wet he could scarcely swallow for several days.

And now My Dear Sister I do not wish you to become discouraged at any reverses we may meet with nor let your spirits run wild at our success within. Either shows a want of firmness that should mark & characterize us who are struggling for all that makes life worth living, for if it should be our fortune to meet with success in the coming campaign let your heart go out to Him who is the Author of all good gifts in thanks and praise; not jubilant, for remember that our success is paid for by the life blood that shall leave some hearth stones vacant and should we meet with reverse, Oh! Let your heart bow with humble submission to the chastisement, still never losing faith that we will eventually triumph over our Enemys. I tell you My Dear Sister that however dark and gloomy the clouds may look above us, seeming just ready to break and overwhelm us in one chaos of rain, they hide behind them the smiling face of an offended God. The clouds are skirted with silver lining and the rainbow of hope still spans the Heavens to the eyes of the faithful.

Our ship of state is freighted with the hopes and prayers of the noblest women the world ever saw and she cannot nor will not be stranded. Your prayers will move the arm of her helmsman to guide her into the port of national security where she will take her place among the nations of the Earth as Gods chosen people and bless the world with her council. We can never yield. The bleaching bones of a hundred thousand gallant comrades as ever trod the soil would rise and shake their gory fingers and cry shame upon us. Their tongues would be clothed in living fire to curse to eternal infamy the man who would whisper 'yield.' There is honor in extermination but dishonor, disgrace and eternal degradation follow in the train of submission. The serfs of Russia would be a happy people compared to our condition with the yankee black Republican for our lord and task master.

And now, my Dear Sister, there is another thing I would warn you against. When you write to any of us or to any one with whom you may be in correspondence in the army, try and let your letters breathe a spirit of cheerfulness and patriotism. You know not how it cheers our hearts to get cheerful letters from loved ones at home and how equally depressing it is to get letters that breathe a spirit of discontent.

I tell you, Sister Scottie, that one half of the desertions from the southern Army is caused by the letters they receive from mistaken friendship at home. We would all like to be at home yet we know and felt that our first and highest duty is to the God who made us and who has preserved and who has redeemed us. Our next duty is to our country because to it we owe our liberty, our right of property, our laws and our society. And last, though not least, is the duty which we owe to ourselves and to our family. I am sorry to say that some of the Texas Rangers have forsaken their colors and have gone home; among them Cousin Jim

McGuire.[102] They have acted very wrong in a three- fold sense. First they acted wrong in forsaking the Regt. at a time when we needed every man to assist us in sustaining ourselves in East Tennessee. Then they acted very wrong in violating their pledged faith of honor that they would return at the expiration of forty days and that they would not attempt to cross the Enemy's line. Third they have acted in bad faith to the Regt. We could get furloughs in order to get summer clothing but now we are deprived of the privilege and a stain is cast upon the whole Regt. by the action of those who have gone home. If I should come home under such circumstances I feel that I would deserve to be driven from home and if I know you, my sister, I think you would rather drop the tear over me in an honorable grave than to receive me with a stain upon my name. And although those boys have not deserted and gone to the enemy, they have deserted their colors and left their comrades in arms here to bear the burden. Their names will be published and handed down to posterity through the records of the country as Deserters.

I was once in hopes that we would be transferred to the Transmissippi Dept. but now I am willing to confess that I do not wish to see the Regt. on that side of the River and were it left to a vote I would certainly vote against it.

My letter has already reached too long a length or I think I could give you satisfactory reasons for what I have just said and in my next I may do so. I know well you think it strange and six months ago if any one had told me I would oppose the Regt. going to Texas I would have told him he was a fool.

And now Dear Scott you must give my love to all inquiring friends.

I forgot to state that your last letter was so badly burned I could only make out a part of it. It was dated Jan 7th. Cousin Cap has received letters up to the 28th. Give my love to Uncle and Aunt

---

102. This was an error, as will later be brought out in the letters. Jim McGuire-was at home on leave, and had not yet returned, due to illness.

Scott, Cousin Pal[103] and to every body end everything that you care for, even to my horse Whangdoodle, and especially to our Dear Mother.

May the Lord watch over you and bless and keep you & us as in the hollow of his hand untill we can all meet honorable is the prayer of your Devoted Brother Bob.

JOHN HILL TO MRS. M. E. BROOKS[104]

I send a few lines to Scott Phillips.[105] Send it to her. I have but one envelope.

Marietta Ga, June 11, 1864

Mrs. M. E. Brooks

Dear Sister

Your thrice welcome letter came to hand a few days since April 15th sent by Mr. Hornsbey. Also two for Bro Tom, one for Cap from Aunt Scott, one for Cousin Bob Hill from Cousin M. Watson.[106] This is the first letter that I have received from any of you since last fall. But still I write by every opportunity that presents itself. This leaves us all well that is here. Bro Bob is at Mareitta in the hospital waiting on the wounded. They have about fifteen hundred of the worse cases from the front there. The others have

103. Cousin Pal was Palmyre A. W. McGehee, the wife of Dr. James Dionysius Oliver of Bastrop County. She now lives in San Marcos.

104. Mrs. M. B. Brooks was Martha Elizabeth Hill, a daughter of Middleton Hill's.

105. Scott Phillips was a cousin of the Hills'.

106. Mary Hill Watson was the daughter of Wylie Hill, and a first cousin of John Hill's. She married John Watson.

been sent farther South. Cousin Geo. McGehee is still in S. C. sick. He was improving very fast when last heard from. We are looking for him up soon. Cousin Tom A. Hill is off wounded. We have not heard from him lately. He is at Forsythe. In my last letter written whilest at Dalton I mentioned the deathe of C. T. Pelham[107] of our Company He was killed on the 9th of last monthe. He was intelligent, high-minded and as brave as ever fell upon any battlefield. J. H. Cheshier was also wounded through the hand just after we had come out of the fight by his horse knocking down Tom Taylors gun which was by a tree. He had to have his hand taken off. He is off somewhere at a hospital. He was a good soldier and a good man. When I wrote last at Dalton I had no idea that our army was going to fall back but the Enemy did not choose to give us battle but rather to flank. We have got the best of every fight that we have had with them. They report their loss since they commenced to advance to be thirty thousand whilest ours is not over ten thousand if that many. We went around in their rear and attack them at Casvill on the 24th of last monthe. We took about two hundred prisoners, about the same number of waggons of which we burned about one hundred and brought the rest off. G B. Burk of our Company was wounded slightly in the shoulder. John M Claiborne[108] was wounded in the arme, not serious. We had seven wounded in the Regt. Some of them severe but none of them that you know. Since the night of the 26th we have been dismounted and in the ditches nearly all the time. There has been more or less fighting every day but the Enemy up to the present time have failed to advance upon our breastworks except at some point along the lines and they have been very easily repulsed. When ever they do fight, which I hope will be very soon, I think you will hear a good account from us for our men are all right. I have just returned from the other side of the Etawa River. T.

107. C. T. Pelham was from Travis County
108. John M. Caliborne was from Travis County.

A. Gill,[109] I and six others crossed the river on the fourth of this monthe and went up in the neighborhood of Calhoon & Adansvill. We were gone seven or eight days in amongst the Yanks, all the time watching them. They are running the cars to the Etawa River. I went over there to try to get Dr. Bob a horse as he is afoot but did not succeed. We did not fall in with any small squads of the Enemy but saw plenty of them. There is some deserters over there, most of them from the 3rd Ga Cavalry. Some of them have taken the Oathe. It is hard that we have to fight a Nation of twice our numbers, recruited from the old world, the Negroes that fall into the federal hands and some of our own people with them. I do not believe there is a state in the South but they have got more or less from where they have got a foot hold.

But Dear Sister I am sorry to hear through some of the boyes that some of the people of Texas are getting dispondant. But thanks to God I have not received any such letters from any of you. Shall we give it up after so many of our bravest & best men have fallen? No, never. They may over run us for a time withe their emmense Armies but they will never whip us. We have whipped them in Va, West of the Miss. River and we will whip them here whenever they fight. They may flank till we get back to the Chatahoocha River this side of Atlanta but they will have to fight some time. And the father they get South, the worse it is for them. The crops here looks fine. Corn is about knee high. Wheat & barley, rye & oats all looks fine and will soon be ready to harvest. The fruit crops will be good. We received a letter several dayes ago from Uncle Wm. Gresham. They were all well except Aunt Emley. She was improving.

We have heard through a yankey prisoners that was taken by some of the Regt. that there was one of the Rangers in Nashvill that had taken the oathe and was married to a Lady from Ky. He described Bob Hill but had forgot the name. When asked if his name was Hill he said that he believed it was. I will never believe

109. T. A. Gill was from Bastrop County.

this till I know it to be true. I see that Cousin M. Watson says that none of us have ever written to any of them. I have written to her and to Uncle Wiley bothe since Bob has been gone and I know that Bro Bob wrote to them.

My love to all and axcept the same for you & yours. Kiss the children for me.

Your Devoted Bro,
Jno. W. Hill

JOHN W. HILL TO MARY SCOTT HILL

Camp West of Marietta
Three miles on of Infantry June 26, 1864

Miss Mary. S. Hill
Bastrop

Dear Sister

I wrote to Sister Matt a few dayes ago. But as Capt. Littlefield of Company "I" of this Regt. is going to start to Texas next Monday I thought I would not fail to write. This leaves us all well. Bro Bob is still at Marietta in hospital. I received a letter from Cousin Geo McGehee a few dayes ago. He said that he had got almost well and would be up in a few dayes. Frank received a letter a few dayes ago from Cyntha Walker.[110] She said that all of the relations were well. Dear Sister I have done a great deal of hard service but since the 4th of May, the time we left Resaca, we have been on the pad all the time. Sometimes in the ditches, sometimes build-

110. Cyntha Walker was a relative of Mrs. Middleton Hill's. The "relations" mentioned were from Alabama.

ing breastworks. Have been on three raids in the rear of the Enemy. The last was much the hardest. We were gone ten dayes. We went to Cleveland in Tenn. We were on our horses nearly all the time, night and day.

Major Christian was in Command with about two hundred of the best mounted men of our Regt. We took some torpedoes along to put under the Railroad. I have not heard yet what damage they done the enemy but hope they blowed the engine and trains loaded with troops on the other side of Jordan or some worse place. Whilest we were on the trip I stopped to get some fodder for my horse and as I was passing Company "E" one of the men was leading an old half-starved yankey horse. The horse made a grab at the fodder which I had tied before me and he got hold of my leg and like to have taken out a piece. Since then I have been so lame I can hardly walk. For that reason I am not in the ditches today with the rest of the Company. One of Company "B" was killed yesterday. His name was King. He was sitting down under a Gin–House rubbing his pistol and was shot by one of the Enemys Sharp Shooters. The ball entered his breast and came out his back. He had not been withe the Regt. a great while. He was from Tennessee. We have never got a chance at the enemy as yet from breastworks but if we do I think we will show them that we can do as good work there as on horseback. There is not a Cavalry Regt. in the Yankey army in this Department. The Enemy show no disposition to give us battle but are throwing up works in front of ours. The skirmishes in many places are very close together. And night & day they keep up a constant fire withe now and then the boom of a cannon. Sometime the musketry rattles away as if they had began in good earnest. Our batteries on top of Kenisaw Mountain are firing now.

Crops here look very well. The corne is from knee to hip high. Wheat is ripe and ready for harvest. Oats, barley and all other small grains look well. The fruit crop bids far to be good. In all the old fields there is thousands of Dubaries [dewberries] which is a great treat to a soldier. The soldiers dessert will soon be ripe.

There has been more rain this Spring than I ever saw before. It rained for nearly two monthes. But at present the weather is very dry and hot. The news from Va is very little. Grant seems to be trying to get Petersburg but Genl Beauregard is there and he whipped Grant once. I think withe a little help from Gen. Lee he will do it again.

We have not heard anything from Cousin Tom Hill since he left. They are going to start withe the letters in a few minutes so I must close. Others of the boyes would have written had they known it in time.

Your Brother,
Jno W. Hill

P. S. Give my love to all and axcept the same yourselfe. Bro Tom is well and would have written had he known it in time.

JOHN W. HILL TO MARY SCOTT HILL

Camp at Covington Ga, Aug 7, 1864

Miss M. S. Hill
Bastrop

Dear Sister

As we are in camp this morning I thought I would drop you a few lines to let you know that we are all well. We have just returned from the left wing of our army. We went over there after a raid on the Enemy. We first caught up with them at Jonesburough on the Atlanta & Macon Railroad where we had a fight with them. They had done very little damage to the Railroad when we came up withe them. They withdrew there forces after night in the direction of Newman, Coweta Co. We caught up withe their rear guard at Shake–Rag, a little place between Fayettesvill & Newman and captured about 150 prisoners and killed several. I am sorry to informe you that in the fight Major Thornton of Company F was killed. He was shot in the face and killed dead. I was close to him but did not see him fall but do not think he ever spoke. He was a good soldier and a brave man and ought to have had a good position in the army but he never sought it. After riding all night and nearly all of two dayes we came up to them again about 3 miles from Newman. Our Regt & the 4th Tenn was dismounted. We drove them a short distance when they gave us such a heavey volley that we had to fall back. Then Ross's Texas Brigade came to our assistance and we drove them from the field. I captured a prisoner and had taken him back & delivered him to the guard, which was near our horses, when the Enemy made a charge on our horses which had been left without any support. I mounted my horse and with about ten or twelve others kept them back untill they could get off with the horses. We had very few men in the fight as we had ridden so hard that a great many of our horses had given out. We had two killed and ten or twelve wounded in the Regt. V. Catron[111] of our Company was wounded in the leg We killed and wounded about 150 of the Enemy and captured about one thousand. And got nearly all of their horses. We got two pieces of artillery, some waggons & ambulances. I got a Six Shooter and a Spencer Gun which shoots 7 times. But as I had two Six Shooters before I let Bro Tom have the pistol. Bro Tom got him a very good horse.

Bro Bob is at East Point in the hospital. We saw Cousin Tom Hill about two weeks ago. He was well. Cousin Cap got a mule in the fight and went down to Griffen. He left his horse and is riding the mule. He got back last night. All is well down there. Cap got a letter from S. Blanton last night. She is down at Uncle Billys.

111. V. Catron was from Travis County.

They are all well down there. H. Williamson is in State Service. After the fight was over at Newman I got a pass and went to see Mrs. Honeycutt, Mr. Parks'[112] second wife. She had just got a letter from Cousin John Parks. He is sick in the hospital at Petersburg Va. I stayed one night withe them. They asked a thousand questions about you all. She has two daughters. One was married but her husband died in the army. She has one child. The other daughter is a young lady, a very nice girl. She had two sons in the armey one of them is dead. I also called on John Hill's[113] family in Newman. He is Col. of a Regt. of State troops. Burwell Hill lost his arm by a wound received at Getteysburg. He was at home but I did not get to see him. He lives some distance from town. Frank McGuire got a letter a few days ago from Cynthia Walker.[114] She reports all well down there. She says she will go to Texas withe us after the war is over if we will go by after her. But I am afraid that time will never come. There is a report in the Regt. that there will two officers be sent from the Regt. this winter after the men that have gone home from the Regt. We are resting at this place for a few dayes. I expect in less than a week we will turne up in the rear of the enemy. The Enemy made a raid to Macon whilest we were after the other raid but they did not get off much better than the ones that we were after, as they got Gen. Stonemon and about half of his command. Crops here is fine. We have roasting ears for breakfast, dinner & supper. Fruit crop is very good. But how I long to be at home and rest where the sound of the bugle will not arouse me nor the sound of artillery & musketry will not disturb my repose. Scott I feel like I could write a week if I knew that this would ever reach you. But I have written so much and yet no answer returns that I almost dispair of ever hearing from home any more. All the boyes are well. There is nothing new or

112. Mr. Parks married Mary Hill, who was a sister of Middleton Hill. Mary Hill died and he married Mrs. Honeycutt.
113. John Meriwether Hill was a second cousin of Middleton Hill's. Burwell Hill was John Meriwether Hill's brother.
114. See Note 111.

strange. You must excuse all mistakes and write often and long letters for you do not know how much I want to hear from home. Cousin Geo McGehee has gone withe Lt Black to the rear of the Enemy after horses.

All join me in much love to you all.

Your Brother,
Jno W. Hill

ROBERT EDWARD HILL TO MARY SCOTT HILL

East Point Ga, August 8, 1864

Sister Mary,

As I have an opportunity to write you a few lines this morning I embrace it gladly.

I am in good health and all the boys in the Regt that you are acquainted with I believe are doing very well.

I have been ordered to assist in hospital for the entire cavalry corps and I have not seen Brother Tom, Brother John & Cousin Cap for some time. I hear from them occasionally and they are all well. Cousin Tom Anderson was wounded at Resaca in the foot. He was absent from his command about one month and is back again with his command. He went to see Uncle Billy and Aunt Emily while he was wounded. Tom was in fine health when I saw him a few days ago. The Col. is waiting and so are the Cors.

Give my love to everybody and accept the same for yourself.

From your Dear Brother,
Bob

JOHN W. HILL TO MARY SCOTT HILL

Camp Near Florence Ala
Sept 15, 1864

Miss M. S. Hill
Bastrop

Dear Sister

I wrote to you a few dayes before we started on this trip And sent it through by one of the 3rd Arkansas. I also wrote to Sister Matt by Capt Kyle a few dayes ago. But as one of the 4th Texas is here that is wounded and is going to start home in the morning I thought I would write to you a few lines. This leaves us all well. Brother Tom went off a few dayes ago to have his horse shod and one of the boyes that came in last night says he has gone to Aberden Miss to visit our relations on a French furlow. There has been about twenty or thirty of the 3rd Arkansas Regt. left for some since we got back on this side of the river. Also some of the 11th Texas and there may be some of our Regt. gone the same way.

If so I hope they will never come back and that their names will be sent through so they can be published as Deserters, for Atlanta has fallen into the hands of the Enemy. Our army has been forced back and now is the time that we need every man, and the men that leaves at such time as this is no man at all. Cap was sent off on duty yesterday morning and is not in Camp. Lt G. M. Dechard[115] came back to the Company this morning. He has been on Col Harrisons staff. This is the most desolate looking country you ever saw; lots of famlies that were wealthy before this war now have not got a pound of meat. Their Negroes are all gone, their fencing all burned and many of their houses. All their stock has been taken. And the country stands a desolate waste.

---

115. G. H. Decherd was from Bastrop County.

Some of the boyes went to see W. H. Caldwell[116] yesterday. He is getting along very well. I hope that he will soon be well again and that his wound will prove nothing serious. We have not heard any thing from our relations since my last letter to you all. We are, it is said, resting here for a few dayes for another raid into Tennessee and that Gen. Forest is going with us.

I got a good pair of boots, a hat, two Six Shooters, three horses and saddles. The horses I gave to the Company. I sold the saddles for fifty dollars a piece. Got a silver watch for which I took fifty-five dollars in green back. Scott you may think this is robbing them but you do not know as much about the yankeys as I do. I have seen them take the last cent from our boyes and they would have taken mine when they had me if they could. I also got three pocket knives. I shot one fellow in the back not more than five feet from him and he fell from his horse but I did not stop to see whether is died or not but run on till I had shot out every load and then got three prisoners.

My love to all.

Your Bro,
John. W. Hill

116. W. H. Caldwell was from Bastrop County. He was wounded September 7, 1864.

JOHN W. HILL TO MARY SCOTT HILL

Camp near Jacksonville Ala
Oct 29, 1864

Miss M. S. Hill
Bastrop

Dear Sister

I wrote a long letter to Sister Matt. And expected to send it by Mr. Garrett but as I did not think he would start so soon I sent by the mail to the Mongomery Advertiser to be sent through by Major Adams. We are all well this morning. We crossed the Goosey River day before yesterday and came to this place to guard I suppose against raids of the enemy. We have not heard anything from the army since they started across the mountains. All of the relations were well when I last heard from. We lost our flag that was sent to us by the Ladies of Nashvill. They had stopped and rolled it up and while going through the brush it pulled off and they did not miss it for some time afterwards. The yankeys got it the next day. They found it in the woods. We regret losing it very much as it was a beautifull flag and as it was presented to us by the Ladies of Tennessee[117]

J. R. Ford[118] of our company has been wounded since I wrote to Sister Matt. He was shot through the hand. I do not think he will lose it. Bro Bob is with the Regt. now. He is fat as a bear. Bro Tom[119] left the Regt. in North Alabama and, as we have not heard a word from him since, I suppose that he has gone to Texas. Tell

117. The loss of the flag was a source of regret to the Terry Rangers. It was returned to the Regiment in 1898. In L. B. Giles' *Terry's Texas Rangers*, 91, there is a letter from J. J. Wiler, a Yankee officer who found the flag. His description of the finding of the flag bears cut the details given in this letter.

118. J. R. Ford was from Travis County.

119. Thomas Hill had gone to Aberdeen, Mississippi, where he was visiting some of his relatives by the name of Strong. While there, he was taken very ill, and this accounts for his delay in returning. He later rejoined his regiment, and remained with it until the end of the war.

him if he is there that I did not think he would go off without letting me know where he was going. We have made application for furlows for the whole Regt to go home this winter. I do not have much hopes of ever getting to Texas untill the war is over which I am afraid will be a long time from present prospects. If we do get off I want you have plenty to eat. And tell all the young ladies to look out, for the boyes all say they are going to marry. That is, of course, if they can get the girls consent. Scott I heard that there was a young conscript going to see you. Have you lost all your patriotism? Send him off to the war and tell him to wait untill the war is over, for I would not give a cent for a man that would not serve his country. I also heard that Bro Mid[120] wanted to go into service. Tell him for me that he had better stay at home and go to school and trye to impress his time the best he can untill he gets a year or two older. Most of boyes of his age do not stand the service like older men. Nat Rives is with the waggons on a lame horse. I have not seen E. John[121] for a long time. I believe he is also withe the waggons. Frank, Cap, Geo McGehee, Sam & Jno Watkins[122] all well. And all the boyes of your acquaintance are well. We have received a great many letters from home lately. Some from Uncle Tom, Aunt Scott,[123] Cousins Pal,[124] Henry Oliver, Molly Watson,[125] Sister Matt, Scott Phillips,[126] yourselfe and several others. Some of them written in 1863 but they were all very interesting to us. Bro Bob sent a letter from Cousin Bob Hill to me home. I did not get to see the letter but am very glad that he sent it. Hope that it may reach home safely. It was written from Rock–island, Illinois. I have answered it. Hope that it may not

120. Brother Mid was Middleton Hill, Junior. He was at this time about seventeen years of age.
121. E. Johns lived in Hill's Prairie.
122. George McGehee, Sam and John Watkins were from Hayes County.
123. Uncle Tom and Aunt Scott were Mr. and Mrs. T. B. J. Hill.
124. Cousin Pal—see note 104.
125. Moly Watson—see not 107.
126. See note 106.

be long before him and Cousin Tom are bothe released. It is very humiliating to a man withe any pride to be shut up in a northern prison withe but little room to take exercise, mixed up withe a thousand different kinds of people and withe as many lice; as much filthe and dirt as to almost make a man sick to look in one much less spend a many long winter day withe but little fire and poorly clad. But I hope that something may turn up to shorten their stay and that they may soon be permitted to return to their homes and friends there to spend many a happy hour around the family firesides relating the many trials through which they have passed. Cousin Sue Blanton[127] also received a letter from Cousin Tom McGuire & I think Tom. Bob sent to Uncle Tom. He is at Johnson Island, a prison for the officers.

I will send this in a letter that Cap has written, as envelopes are rather scarce and as I am willing for all to read. The weather is warm and clear withe cold nights. You must give my love to all the relations and friends and axcept the same for yourself. Write often and long letters.

Your Bro,
John W. Hill

John W. Hill to Mary Scott Hill

Grahamsville S. Carolina, Jan 7, 1865

Miss Mary S. Hill
Bastrop

Dear Sister

Many months has passed sinse I attempted to write home and I have no assurance that this will ever reach you. We wrote many letters in North Ala. Since that time we have been on duty all the

127. See note 87.

time and we have not had any opportunity to write. After we left North Ala. we were ordered to Atlanta. But before we got there Sherman commenced his advance through Georgia. The first place that we had any fighting withe him was at Macon on 10th & on the 12th at Grisleville, the first station below Macon. We had a considerable fight. We took about eighty prisoners & killed twenty or thirty. T. J. Watkins of our Company was wounded slightly in the left arm. Lt Friend of Company E was also wounded and several others, their names I do not remember. We then rode night and day, and swam one River to get in Sherman's front which was accomplished at Sandersville where we had a rather considerable fight. Adde Moore of Company H was killed and several others wounded. I got two prisoners, a good overcoat & one hundred dollars in Green–Back, fifty of which I gave to Bro Bob to send to Cousins Tom & Bob Hill. We have not heard any thing from either of them since the last letters that we wrote. We then started after Kilpatrick who had started on a raid in the direction of Augusta. We first caught up withe him at Waynesbourough on the 24th Nov and on the 25th at BuckHead–Church where we rioted him and took a good many prisoners & killed a good many. There S. Wynn of our Company fell. He was from Burleson County and as brave and true a soldier as ever fell in his Countrey's defence. The same day, late in the evening, we came upon them again where they had put up good breastworks out of rails where they intended to spend the night. The 3rd Arkansas Regt. was ordered to charge and we were formed in squadrons to support them. We were in an and open field whilest the 3rd Ark was by fours in the road when the bugle sounded the charge. On we went like Mezepha on his Wild Horse. The Enemy held their fire untill we got about one hundred and fifty yards and then turned loose on us. They had a battery of eight guns. I have been a great many hard places but this was the worst I ever saw. Grape canister shell & solid shot whistled through the air and ploughed the ground in every direction whilest the Minneys came more like a swarme of bees than anything else. We got right up to the breastworks but did not take them. But the enemy left them as soon as we fell back and we did not come up withe them any more untill they got back to there Infantry. Dave Mackle of Company K was killed and several wounded but I do not see how. It looks like they ought to have killed every man. The 3rd Arkansas lost a great many. We then went back to the bridge over Briar Creek to guard the road to Augusta while Sherman passed. We had a fight on the 3rd of December and on the 5th we had a fight at Waynesbourough. D. D. Nunn & T. R. Kennedy of our Company were killed They were as good soldiers and as brave men as ever fell and their relations and friends at home have the sympathies of the Company. If we continue to fight like we have for the last few months but few will ever reach home of this little band to tell the sad tale. We left Macon withe about one hundred & fifty fighting men and since that time we have had thirty men killed & wounded. We followed old Sherman to within 10 or 15 miles of Savannah where the roads got so bad that it was impossible to follow him any father. We then went up and crossed the Savannah River and went down within sight of Savannah to cover the retreat of our forces from that place. We then stayed there and picketed the River untill yesterday when we moved up to this place to rest and be paid off. Cousin Cap Hill's horse gave out while we were after Kilpatrick. He went up to Oglethorpe after his horse and I have not heard from him since but look for him in every day. This is the worst country we have had to soldier in yet. After we left Macon we went a monthe without a bite of bread & we have had but little since that time. Potatoes & pork and sometimes very little of that. We have had but little to feed our horses on except rice but plenty of that. The country is low and flat but little else but fine timber. The roads are all thrown up and to get off of there is to get into a bog for it rains nearly every day. We have given up all hopes of getting home this winter or untill the War is over. We have had little or no cold weather. Bro Bob got a letter from Georgia Strong which informed us that Bro Tom had gone to Texas. Hope that he may have a pleasant time of it. Tell him I got his old mare and left my horse as he was so lame he could not travel. And that I got the old mare wounded but it did not hurt her. This is the fifth horse I have had killed or wounded.

Jan 7, 1865

Miss Mary S. Hill
Bastrop

Dear Sister

I thought that I would finish my letter on the five pages but I have a house in which to write for we are encamped in houses built of pine logs where the 3rd S. Carolina Cavalry have been camped for two years picketing on the coast four miles from this place. They were kind enough to leave us a table to write upon and, as I have nothing else to do but call the Roll and make the detail, I will continue to write. When we got to LeGrange Ga on our way from North Ala. I got a pass to go to Newmon after Brother's mare which I had left withe Mrs. Honeycutt. When I got there I found cousin J. J. Parks[128] at home. He had come home on furlow from Va. I stayed withe them three dayes. They have always treated me as kindly as they could. You can say to Aunt Evie[129] the first time you see her that Mr. North's family were all well when I was there. We have had more sickness since we have been in this country than at any other time since we come in service. J. B. Rector[130] & A. J. Kyle[131] of our Company are sick

128. See note 113
129. Aunt Evie was Mrs. Wylie Hill.
130. J. B. Rector was from Bastrop County.
131. A. J. Kyle was from Hayes County.

but neither of them dangerous. Nat Rives of Company F is also sick but I do not think it is anything serious. They have all been sent of to a private house. Geo T. McGehee was left in N. Alabama on a scout and on his way to the Regt. whiles on the other side of the River, he fell in withe one of Gen. Hardys staff and went withe him on a scout. They run into the Enemy and George lost his horse and every thing on him. The Enemy drove the swamp for him and at one time got very close to him but he got away from them without being seen. There is nothing new or strange here that would interest you. We hear that Gen. Hood has fallen back to the Tennessee River. There is nothing new from Va. The people and some of the soldiers are subjugated but we must never give up the ship. Some times when I see our cavalry whipped and driven back by the Enemy, we have to come to the front to hold them in check untill they can get away. Such was the case at Waynesburough where D. Nunn[132] & Kennedy[133] fell. It makes my heart sink and I am almost ready to give it up, for it is always the best soldiers and the bravest men that fall. And if we gain our independance how few are the numbers that can lay their hands on their hearts and say that they done all they could for their bleeding Country. Some hang around the waggons, some are allways away from there commands, some shirk out on little details and some go withe their commands but when the balls begin to flye, they always have some excuse to go to the rear and when it comes to the fighting men there's that one always there. They are few. Yes, I am sorry to say it...too few. A great many of our cavalry are not worthe the provisions that they consume. They will not fight and are worse to plunder the Country than the yankes are. The enemy committed many outrages on their raid through Georgia, too horrible for me to write. They took a great many Negroes. Many got away and came back to their home the most wretched looking objects I ever saw. Many the Yankeys took along for a few

132. D. Nunn lived across the river from the Kills in Bastrop County.
133. Kennedy was from Bastrop County.

dayes untill their feet got so sore that they could not walk and then turned them loose without anything to eat to travel back over a country that they have stripped of everything to live upon. They killed everything from a chicken up. The bugle has sounded the 'saddle up' and we are looking for it to give us the 'mount your horse' to go where? That is something we never know until we get there. I must close by saying that Dr. Bob,[134] Frank, Geo McGehee, Sam Watkins and all your Relations and friends are well. You must give my love to all the relations and friends and axcept same for yourselfe.

Your Brother,
John W. Hill

P. S. Say to Bro Tom if he intends coming back I would like to have a saddle. If he can manage any way to bring it a Mexican hat and a pair of spurs. I have plenty of money. I have about two hundred in Con–fed, fifty in Green Backs which is worthe ten to one in Con–fed. If they pay us off and I get what is owing to me, I will have about a thousand dollars and that is as much money as I want here. You can say to Ma that I have plenty of clothing such as they are they are coarse but good enough for a soldier. Plenty of blankets. Tell the negroes all howdey for me. You must excuse all mistakes and write soon and a long letter. Tell Sister Matt that I will write to her soon.

As Ever your Bro,
John W. Hill

134. Dr. Bob was Robert Hill. Frank was Frank McGuire.

Robert Edward Hill to Mary Scott Hill

Grahamsville South Carolina
January 8, 1865

My Dear Sister

It has been a long time since I had an opportunity to write to you. And even now I do not know when or how I shall get this started to you. We have been in very active duty ever since Genl. Sherman started from Dalton Ga and more especially since he left Atlanta. We have been fighting him all the way through Georgia. The people would not respond to the call of the Authorities. A great many stayed at home and Sherman was allowed to walk over the track almost without opposition except from the cavalry. I made out a few days ago a list of casualties and sent it on to Parson Bunting who is now at Auburn Hospital in Alabama. I suppose that he will send it on to be published in Texas. You will see that by that list that our Regt has lost very heavily and especially Company D but the Good Lord in his wonderful Mercy has still continued his protecting kindness over us and we are still spared. Brother John has just obtained a leave of absence of ten days and will go to see Aunt Emily and Uncle Billy. Cousin Cap left us as we were coming down in the track of Sherman for the purpose of going to Uncle Billys after a horse & for Crockett who has been staying at Aunt Emileys ever since Cousin Tom was captured at Atlanta. Cap has not yet rejoined his command. Cousin Frank McGuire has been with the command in every fight but is safe & sound and in fine health. Cousin George McGehee is with us and is in good health. We have been trying for some time past to get the Regt all furloughed but Shermans advance through Georgia has for the present suspended all exertions. However, Ex Gov. Lubbock and The Hon. Mr. Reagan have promised to use every exertion to get the Regt. furloughed. And Maj. Gen. Wheeler, who is in command...has pledged himself in our favor and has endorsed to the War Dept. that if we are furloughed he will stand security that the Regt. will return. I think perchance so soon as the storm lulls a little that perhaps we may get them. I suppose before this reaches you will have been surprised by Brother Tom's return home. I was not with the command when Brother left and did not know what to think when I received a letter from Cousin Georgia Strong telling me that Brother has been there and was then on his way to the Transmissippi. I could hardly believe it for a time but hope that he has reached home in safety & that he will return with Maj. Christian & Capt. Kyle. If he does there will nothing be done or said. But if not the consequence will be on his own head and the stigma upon the whole family. I have not heard anything more from Cousin Tom Anderson nor from Cousin Bob. In fact I have had no letters from any one in I don't know when and have had no chance to write since Genl. Sherman began moving from Atlanta untill the present time. We are now in South Carolina and where we will go next I am unable to tell you at this time or what will be the movements of the Armies. Gen. Hood is out of Tennessee and is now at Corinth where Gen. A. Sidney Johnson was when he moved to the Field of Shiloh nearly three years ago. God Grant that Gen. Hood may move to a more glorious victory. Gen. Lee seems to be holding his own in Va. but Sherman has certainly had his own way here in this Dept. The people of Georgia seemed to have become paralized and set down at home and put all upon President Davis to come to their help. I was astonished to find so many men at home and they never came to the rescue. Gen. Sherman ought to have been totally defeated and ruined. But the sad fact will be handed down to posterity that while Sherman's minions were devastating the country with fire & committing all kind of outrages upon defenceless women, the men of Georgia stayed at home, or at least a large portion of them, trying to save what they had and many of them voluntarily took the oath of allegiance to the Government that a little while before they had denounced as every thing mean and despicable. But such is human nature. I thought at one time that Richmond Va would have been given up to capture & destroy Sherman and I believe it would have been very much better for us to have done so. But I must confess that the movements of the Armies now upon the chessboard of War are too complicated for me to see through them. We had to fight Sherman alone with the Cavalry and we lost some of the best men in the Regt. and all for no good. D. D. Nunn & P. R. Kennedy were killed from Company D near Waynesboro Georgia where we fought the whole of Sherman's Cavalry and a division of Infantry. Wm. Nicholson, poor fellow, fell while gallantly fighting them near Rome Georgia on the 13th of October. Our Regt. is now in very good health but unused to such a country as this. I do not know how long this will continue. The water here is very bad indeed and the entire country is, you may say, a marsh—low, very flat—so much so that the water scarcely runs off even when it rains. In fact this is the rice region of South Carolina between here & Savannah.

Well Scottie I have trod upon the soil where Marion trod and have rode over ground where Marion led his chosen band of heroes and have stood beside the tomb where sleeps some of the Heroes of the Revolution of 1776 and I have no language to convey to you my feelings I felt. That I was in the presence of those who struggled as we are now struggling I felt almost that I ought to pull off my shoes for the place ought to be sacred. I have seen one of the pieces of artillery that Marion captured from the British at Purysburg. It is old and nearly eat up with rust. Purysburg was once in the early settlement of this country a flourishing place numbering nearly 8,000 inhabitants. It was once a Welch colony but now it is old, dilapidated with but few houses standing. One would ride through it and never know unless told thus it is. Time makes sad changes with things and places as well as men and nations.

Well Scottie it is now verging on 4 years since I left home and this struggle seems no nearer the end than it did at that time. But still what else can we do than struggle on leaving our cause in the hands of Him Who Doeth all things well, doing our duty and leaving the rest to God. All the boys are very anxious to get home to see loved ones once more but our first duty is to the God who made us. Our next duty is to our Country and our Country needs us now and here. We must stand at our post now that the dark clouds are towering and seem ready to break over us. If every man would do his duty & now come to the rescue it would not be long before the Heart of the Country would be made glad, on account of victory & I think every woman should use all her influences to get men to perform their duty. If the women in the whole South would know the fate that awaits them should we be subjugated let them learn from those who have fallen in the Yankee lines. I think then that they would learn to look upon those who desert their colors with less favor. I felt very much mortified when I learned that the troops in the TransMissippi Dept. had refused to cross the River and come over here and helps us. Had Gen. Hood had two Divisions more of infantry or even one he would have taken Nashville and would have ruined Thomas' Army. Then we would have obtained many recruits in Tenn and also would have been able to have gone into Ky. But we did not have the men. Your side of the River is comparatively quiet while we are struggling here against heavy odds and it does seem to me that they have committed a very great blunder in refusing to cross the River; it would be very much preferred for Texas to fight her battles here in Georgia than to have to fight them upon the soil of Texas...or even La or Arkansas...the farther we fight them from our homes the better. And fighting the battles here we are certainly to some extent fighting for Texas. We may not live here as well as the troops do over there and perhaps do not have as many good clothes to wear and I am sure that we do not get to hear from home often. All of this I will allow. Still we have made out to live for over three years and they might live 6 months or even 12 as we do to gain our independence. We cook our meat on a stick (we get 1/3 pound of bacon or 3/7 of a pound of fresh beef) & bake our bread on a board. Sometimes we do not see a cooking vessel for weeks. Now however they are issuing corn meal. We have a pack for the Company and the boys carry a skillet or two along to bake bread. And since I am acting Surgeon of the Regt. I can carry mine in my ambulance. I am worse off now for clothes & boots than I have ever been. My boots are nearly worn out. They are in the water untill I am not much better off than if I were bare footed and my pants—well no point saying anything about them. I hardly think you would know your Brother were you to meet him in the road. Brother John will go up to Uncle Billy's and I hope to get a supply soon. Our relations have been very kind indeed to us furnish us with what ever we need when they can get a chance. I have never yet had an opportunity of visiting Oglethorpe or in fact leaving the command. There is always enough to do to keep me constantly on hand and I never make application for leave for I would dislike very much to be denied.

Well now Scott you must say to Uncle Tom & Uncle Wiley that I have $50.00 in Greenback that I am trying to send Tom and Bob. I went the other day to see Maj. Genl Wheeler, who told me he thought he could get it through for me. If they can get it, it would enable them to buy things for their comforts.

Well Scott you must give my love to all inquiring friends, to our Dear Mother to Sister Matt. Tell Matt that I have written to her two or three times. Give my love to Sister Sallie[135] and say to Itasca that Nat has been quite sick with fever but is now improving and unless a relapse takes place I think will be able to be up in a few dayes. He was taken sick while we were at Purysburg and I had to move him three times untill at last I got him to a very comfortable place.

Tell Alice[136] that I have been looking a long time for a letter from her but as yet none has come to hand. Tell her I am anxious to hear from her again. Why don't Nish write to some of us? Tell Ruth[137] that she is not forgotten by us. You can say to Mrs. Shipp that I do not know where Bob is only that I heard he was a Lt. in a company in Mississippi. Tell Mrs. Camp that when I was at

135. Sister Sallie was the wife of Thomas Anderson Hill, a son of Middleton Hill.

136. See note 70.

137. See note 69.

Gadaden I went to visit the falls, spent a very pleasant time with the family who lives there and that they wished to be remembered kindly to her and the Doctor. Give Mrs. Camp my kindest regards.

You must say to Uncle Wiley when you see him not to think unkind of us for not writing to him, for when we get a chance to send we can only send about one apiece as who ever goes would have more than he could manage if we sent more. Therefore I try and write to you as if I was writing to all—giving you all the news and mentioning all in whom you are interested.

January 10th—Col. Rieves of the 11th Texas has just received a furlough and will go to Texas and he has promised to carry a letter for me. The boys are all well today.

Now Scottie tell them all to write and write as often as you can. You know not how anxious we are to hear from you. I have written three times to Uncle Thomas & Aunt Scott but have not had a line from them in so long I don't recollect the dates. Tell Cousin Pally[138] to write me and I would be more than glad to get a letter from Cousin Henry Oliver. Tell all the negroes howdy for me. And accept the best wishes and sincerest love from Your

Brother Bob

138. See note 104.

ROBERT EDWARD HILL TO MARY SCOTT HILL

Jan the 10th—And now my Dear Sister you must tell Cousin Alice that I would have written to her but with so many writing and only a pair of saddle bags to for all of our letters to be carried in I would just write to you and through you to all. Tell Alice to write to me by the return mail and if we can get a chance again I will be sure to write to her.

You must give my love to her tell her to be a good girl, learn fast and learn to play some tunes for me. Tell Cousin Scottie[139] that I have not forgotten her. Give my love to her. You must give love to all. To Mrs. J. G. John and to Mrs. Camp. You can tell Miss Jenny Edmonson that her Brother was well when I last saw him. He is down in Ga with Gen. Wharton. You must tell all the negroes howdy for me. Tell them I would like to get back and see them all once more. I hope they will be good and do everything they can to make Mother comfortable.

And now once more My love to everybody at home who asks after us. You must not become discouraged nor disheartened. The clouds of darkness will blow away and Peace & Plenty once again bless our land.

Continue your daily prayers for our safety and recollect that while you are praying for our safety I may be offering up my prayers for yours.

May we soon meet again around our own fireside and none be missed.

Your Brother,
Bob

139. Cousin Scottie was Scottie Phillips, a cousin of the Hills'.

ROBERT EDWARD HILL TO MARY SCOTT HILL

Our Grand Fathers Place[140]
June the 23, 1865

My Dear Sisters

Having an opportunity of writing and sending by hand, and knowing that you must be very anxious to hear from me I gladly embrace the chance.

I have been here with Aunt & Uncle now about 6 weeks and they have been troubled so much about the Yankee raiding through the country that I have not been away but once and that was a few days ago. I went down to see Cousin Meriwether Hill's[141] family. Found them all in very good health. The yankees have been treating some of the people very bad but up to this time there has been but two in the house here and they were here when Brother Tom[142] was here. Aunty & Uncle have both been sick since Brother Tom left; nothing very serious however. Aunt Emily is failing very fast, ever since I came. They are very anxious for me to stay with them for a while and although I want to get home very much I think I will stay with them untill the travelling facilities are better than they are now. So you need not expect me before Fall. Auntie Speaks often of the boys who have left and gone on home and is very anxious to hear from them. I have not heard one word from them since they left and of course you must know how anxious I feel. My Prayer is that they may have all reached home in safety even before this time.

Well Sister, the War is ended and we are—What—The Future is in the hands of that God who has extended his kindness and protecting power over us during the last 4 years that Death has held its high carnival over all our land. Let us not distrust him.

140. The old Hill home was in Lexington, Georgia.

141. See note 114.

142. This is evidence that Thomas Hill returned to his regiment, and surrendered with the Terry Rangers in North Carolina.

"God moves in a mysterious way
His wonders to perform;
He plants his Foot Steps on the Sea,
And rides upon the storm."

The Future indeed looks dark enough but I must confess that I do not feel as some do...denying our Maker, trampling under foot his divine words and making a mockery of all past.

The States that once seceded are now petitioning through the people in meetings of Counties to return to the Union again, taking upon themselves the yoke and expressing a willingness to wear that yoke for all time to come. Those who stayed at home and refused to come to our help when we were calling now begin to wish they had done a little more, been less anxious to make a few dollars more or save a little more money. We have the mortifying consolation of knowing that he Yankees never could have whipped us if we had only remained true to ourselves. But dissatisfaction became broadcast over the land. Fathers, Mothers, Cousins, Sisters would write to their brothers, sons or cousins in the Army to come home. Speculation was holding its hydra head and riding in fine buggies and carriages while soldiers wives were suffering and almost starving. The dissatisfaction extended to the Army and then began desertion. Desertion & speculation will be written against us in the page of history that records our failure.

The People of the South are not ready for liberty. A few years under the gaoling chains and I think the care of money will be ground out of some of them.

And now Sister you must say to our Dear Mother for me do not feel despondent. The Almighty has had us under protection in answer to her Prayers. And God promises that he will be the husband of the widow and a father to the fatherless with Him to lean upon. Although the future may look dark and stormy and no ray of light to light in the dark vista may appear yet, with the eye of Faith we can look beyond the cloud to the smiling face of him who taught us when we pray to say "Thy Will, Oh Father, not mine be done!"

Say to Uncle Tom & Auntie that I have not heard from Cousin Tom since I was at Fort Delaware. That was the 20th of March. Cousin Tom was well then. I have seen no account of any release of Prisoners from Johnson Island. Tell them I often think of them and hope it will not be a great while before I will again be at home and ready to meet around the family fire side and claim my pipe for a smoke.

Tell Cousin Poll to have an extra supply of sausages for me this Fall, for I want to make up lost time. Tell Miss Ruth—Well—Tell her I want to kiss her Baby. Say to all enquiring friends that I am well and hope to be with them ere the year is ended.

Give my love to all the negroes. Auntie says with tears in her eyes to give you all the love that can be put on paper. She says Brother Tom & John must write to her.

Tell brother Tom that Miss Mary C. says she sometimes thinks of him and dreams of him her sleep.

Say to Cousin Alice that I would write to her but I hope before much longer that I shall have the great satisfaction of talking to her in *propria persona*.

Say to her ten thousand thanks for her tobacco pouch and that I have put it to a more nobler use than holding tobacco. I have put my 4 years' labor and the relic of a ruined Country in it...My one dollar in Specie.

Give my love to all enquiring Friends and for yourselves know that you have the undying love of your Devoted Brother,

Bob

P. S. I write this to both of you I will address to Sister Mary, but I am writing to both.

Bibliography

The Hill Letters are in the Library of the University of Texas.

All the other original documents here used belong to Mr. T. O. Hill of Smithville.

T. J. Hill, *The Hills of Wilkes County, Georgia and Allied Families,* Johnson-Dallas Company, Atlanta, Georgia, 1922.

W. L. Grissom, *Methodism in North Carolina,* two volumes, Publishing House of the M. E. Church, South, Nashville, Tennessee, 1905.

George R. Gilmer, *Early Georgians,* D. Appleton & Co., New York, 1855.

D. G. Wooten (ed.), *A Comprehensive History of Texas,* 1685-1897, two volumes, W. G. Scorff, Dallas, Texas, 1898.

Printed in the United States
222294BV00001B/12/P

9 780982 246719